The Recruiter's
Super Query Blueprint

The Recruiter's
Super Query Blueprint
....
Your Complete Guide for Crafting Effective Search Strings.

Moises Lopez

This publication is designed to provide competent and reliable information regarding the subject matter covered. However, it is sold with the understanding that the author and publisher are not engaged in rendering legal, financial, or other professional advice. Laws and practices often vary from state to state and if legal or other expert assistance is required, the services of a professional should be sought. The author and publisher specifically disclaim any liability that is incurred form the use or application of the contents of this book.

Copyright © 2014 Moises Lopez

All rights reserved. Except as permitted under the U.S. Copyright Act of 1976, no part of this publication may be reproduced, distributed, or transmitted without the prior written permission.

Permission to reproduce or transmit in any form or by any means, electronic or mechanical, including photocopying and recording, or by any information storage and retrieval system, must be obtained in writing from the author, Moises Lopez.

Printed in the United States of America

First Edition: August 2013

ISBN_13:978-1495457371

ISBN-10:1495457370

The Recruiter's
Super Query Blueprint

Your Complete Guide for Crafting
Effective Search Strings.

Moises Lopez

The Recruiter's
Super Query Blueprint

Contents at a Glance

Introduction..i

    Chapter 1. Eight Steps To Crafting Super Search Strings.......1

The First Pillars of search string crafting............................... 14

    Chapter 2. Creating your search objective........................15

The second pillar of search string crafting...........................34

    Chapter 3. Selecting Core Keywords 35

    Chapter 4. Find the right Supporting Keywords.................44

    Chapter 5. Strengthening queries thru Keyword Stemming.55

The third pillar of search string crafting 67

    Chapter 6. Creating word images that target results...........68

    Chapter 7. Integrating words thru strategic positioning......87

The Fourth Pillar of Super Search Strings 99

    Chapter 8. Design the right approach for your query........100

    Chapter 9. Wiping out Irrelevant Results thru exclusions...125

Conclusion..151

About the Author

The Recruiter's
Super Query Blueprint

Table of Contents

Introduction..i
    Chapter 1. Eight Steps To Crafting Super Search Strings.......1
        The Eight Step Process......................................2
        Step 1: Creating A Search Objective 5
        Step 2: Selecting Core Keywords..........................5
        Step 3: Developing Supporting Keywords 7
        Step 4: Upping your game with Concept Stemming!..8
        Step 5: Creating Word Images 9
        Step 6: Integrating Your Keywords.....................10
        Step 7: Taking Charge of your Search Strings 11
        Step 8: Wiping out Irrelevant Results 12
The First Pillars of of search string crafting......................14
    Chapter 2. Creating your search objective........................15
Step 1: Creating A Search Objective..16
        Guiding your search results............................... 17
        Creating great search strings is not about choosing great keywords...18
        Identifying a Search Objective 19
        Defining the core concepts..................................20
        The three concepts 30
        Points to Keep in Mind 31
        Summing up search objectives............................32
The second pillar of of search string crafting........................ 34
    Chapter 3. The Secret to Selecting Highly Effective Keywords 35

Step Two – Selecting Core Keywords 36
   Core Keywords...37
   Identifying your Core Concepts..........................38
   What to do with these keywords........................40
   Wild goose chase proofing your search strings..42

Chapter 4. Keywords with a Supporting Role..................... 44
   Step Three – Finding the Right "Supporting" Keywords..45
      Supporting words are 46
      Databases don't define your words..................49
      Specificity..53

Chapter 5. Not your Traditional Stemming........................55
   Step Four – Strengthening queries thru Keyword Stemming...56
      Harnessing the Power of your Keywords thru Stemming!..57
      An example of "Stemming" keywords................ ..58
      How do we use concept stems?.........................59
      Research your keywords..................................60
      Research is hard...61
      The Importance of Keyword Research.................62
      Awaken your keyword Hunter...........................63
      Summing up Stems... 64

The third pillar of search string crafting 67
   Chapter 6. Creating word images that target results.........68
      Step Five – The Power of putting keywords together... 69
      Evoking a response..70
      Grouping our keywords 72
      An Example of Grouping...................................73
      Grouping Large Numbers of keywords..................74
      Combining Groups...75

Merging Groups.. 76
Complex Nesting... .77
Tips for building complex queries 80
Summing up Groups...81
Chapter 7. Keyword Positioning...................................82
   Step Six – Integrating your words thru Strategic positioning 83
      Why does the position of keywords matter?..........84
      Relevance and your search strings... 85
      Positioning Keywords...88
      Bad Keyword Positioning.....................................89
      Each word carries with it a connotation...............90
      Keyword Positioning in Action............................ 91
      Clever of Positioning Keywords...........................93
      Another example of keyword positioning............94
      Here's the skinny...95
      Keyword Positioning and great results.................96
      Quick ways to Spice up search strings through positioning... 97
      Summing up... 98
The Fourth Pillar of Super Search Strings 99
   Chapter 8. Getting the most out of your search string......100
      Step Seven – Designing the right approach for your query 101
      The real purpose of your search string............... 102
      Effective vs. Super queries 103
      Let's just get started.... 104
      Dealing with Chaotic Results 107
      Identify the right issues 109
      Analyzing our results... 110
      Determine an approach.................................. ...111

The Refinement..112
Editing and testing your query..............................113
Prominence Issues Explained 114
Another way to get around Prominence................115
Why you're going to be better at this
than other Recruiters 117
Maximizing your search string..............................119
Yet another way around prominence....................120
Addressing locations..121
Summing up this chapter.....................................123
Chapter 9.The Real Purpose of Exclusions......................125
Step 8 – Wiping out Irrelevant Results
thru Exclusions... 126
Defining Exclusions...127
Search string surgery 128
Bad results happen because... 129
Exclusion Basics 130
Words of Caution 131
Getting off track 134
How to tell if you're getting off track....................135
How to test your keywords..................................136
Excluding websites 137
The minus sign and advanced commands............138
The Minus Sign and the Site command 140
The difference between all three........................ 141
Excluding Title Tags 142
Word of caution..143
Chapter Summary...144
Conclusion...148
About the Author

Searching is just like finding, only it comes first and is spelled differently.

> Author Unknown

The Recruiter's
Super Query Blueprint
....
Your Complete Guide to Crafting Effective Search Strings.

Moises Lopez

Introduction

The idea for this book was born from a bunch of conversations I had as I was conducting training sessions at Accenture.

Sourcers and Recruiters alike often approached me. Throughout my conversations the recurring topic of conversations was crafting search strings.

The difficult roles that we were constantly being asked to search for made it hard to continuously find candidates.

The Recruiters and Sourcers knew how to search. These were not rookie searchers, yet they struggled to find candidates in our database.

The database had over 700 million profiles so chances were that we had the candidates in our database, yet they still couldn't come up with the candidates they needed.

I would frequently see that even though they had a great collection of tactics, they missed the mark on some of the most important components that make a search strings work.

I spent a lot of time talking search string strategy at Accenture.

I found myself talking about what keywords to use and what went into successfully combining them. We talked about the coolest, most remarkable ways to combine great keywords with smart tactics, about how to put together effective search strategies.

I decided to do more than talk. I decided to put these thoughts together for others who may be going through the same struggles.

Those lessons learned became the "*Recruiter's Super Query Blueprint*". Years ago, I started writing search strings for my new recruiting practice. It wasn't easy; I didn't know much of what I was doing. I would just crank out searches and it seemed like a daunting task at first.

But over the course of twenty years I've become more much more comfortable with searching. I have learned a few valuable lessons along the way.

This book contains some of the core lessons and on the nuts and bolts of what goes into creating your own super search strings.

I've written them in steps that we return to several times, building on what's gone before, so that as you review the lessons with me, you're creating a solid query structure that gives you the best potential

What you'll get out of this book

This book is intended to give you a real grounding in the way to put the components of search string creation together effectively.

In the next few chapters we'll explore the art and science of search strings design. I'll be teaching you many techniques that are pivotal concepts, which you MUST know if you want to write strong search strings that deliver results.

Also, it's important to know that anyone, and I mean ANYONE, can do it.

The information within this book should be quite easy to follow. It will unravel the difficulties of finding candidates and point you in the right direction to succeeding at search.

Through this volume I will layout an easy blueprint for you to understand and follow.

Now in case that you still have questions after reading this book, I want you to contact me with your questions through my personal email: moises@thesourcingcorner.com.

I will personally walk you through each of the steps.

I want Recruiters and Sourcers alike to learn a very realistic way to put together strong effective search strategies.

My purpose is not to make money by selling this book and walk away. That is why I will be around to help guide you through any problems or questions you might have. My goal is to see Recruiters and Sourcers succeed.

I've done it using this exact system.

I know it works because it took me years to figure things out and what I've learned is that there is a RIGHT way and a WRONG way to search.

This blueprint is a system that shows you the RIGHT way to write Super Queries that find candidates.

To find candidates, you need to create a specific search string that manipulates the search algorithms to do things that go against their design.

To do that, you need to understand the multiple elements that come into play and how they can help you reach your target candidates. This means that you have to know what you're doing.

You need to become an expert at search to write good quality search strings so that you can drive results with authority.

You need to surround yourself with research tools that can help you build and grow your keyword knowledge.

My book will give you the specifics on where to focus your attention and will help point out some of the wrong choices that cause Recruiters and Sourcers to fail at their searches.

Databases and search engines are huge playgrounds that are filled with enormous opportunities to find viable candidates.

With over two billion people online and a projection of over five billion by 2020, there are definitely candidates out there that are a great fit for your job and your company.

It is up to you to learn how to best use your search strings to deliver them.

My book will pave the way to help you do just that. I look forward to hearing about your search success!

Chapter One

The Eight Steps for Crafting A Super Query

The Eight-Step Process

How do Recruiters recognize good search strings?

There is a big difference between good and bad queries. Many Recruiters can identify a good one, but they don't know what makes the difference.

Most of them are not looking at a search strings and thinking: "That query has strategic keyword positioning and excellent use of exclusions!"

Nope.

In most cases Recruiter just feel like there is something good about it. Maybe it's the keywords choices or the use of parentheses, but they never actually know for sure. There is something more to good search string crafting than looking right.

So, what more is there?

Effective search string crafting boils down to one thing: defining a clear request to your database in a way that it has no other option but to deliver it.

You don't need a three-year learning curve to learn how to do it. Just take note as you read so you can benefit from the lessons I've learned.

Let's get started...

The common assumption is that searching is largely a matter of about identifying and selecting the right keyword. This assumption creates search strings defined by combinations of keywords, synonyms and the like, and is the basis for what they consider to be well designed queries.

While identifying and selecting keywords is important; it is not nearly enough.

Selecting the right keywords is an important step in the query writing process but it doesn't even rank around the most important steps.

Most of Recruiters will find this statement to be utterly absurd or even crazy.

After all what could be more important than using the right keyword, right?

Not only is it true, it strikes at the core of the sourcing problems today.

When the search strategy is focused on keywords, in a very real sense it becomes an obstacle to finding the right results.

So, if searching is not about the keywords what is it about, then?

To understand "search," it would be helpful to think of searching as the process of coordinating the activities of the algorithms that make up your database or search engine.

That sounds like a mouthful.

Searching is about recognizing that your keywords are only a part of it. They are your tools for delivering a word image that directs the databases to do what you need them to do.

All parts of a query are chain linked to create and deliver these instructions to your database.

Every letter, every space, every symbol used or even omitted, is an instruction to your database. As a result, all affect your results.

Once you understand the principles of search that bind all the pieces together, finding candidates isn't all that difficult.

The difference between the best search results you could ever achieve and the worst; have less to do with the keyword that you choose or the database that you are using.

<u>It has everything to do with how you searched.</u>

It took me years to figure this out. You will learn as well that to communicate with your database your search strings must change.

The following eight steps will guide you in assembling a firm idea of the components of strong search strings, and will focus their incredible problem solving power on a solution for your specific search.

Step 1: Creating A Search Objective

Depending on the type of search you may need to conduct, you may need a different use of keywords, different tools, and different strategies.

One thing remains constant though.

That is, if you want to achieve great results, it starts by deciding what those great results are going to be.

That is why we need a search objective.

The objective provides the context for the search string crafting process. It creates a clear picture of what we need to find by defining the parameters that will hold your search strings together.

By narrowing your search down to a specific objective statement you set your self up to create targeted solutions for your queries.

This is the key element to crafting super search strings.

Step 2: Selecting Core Keywords

The second step deals with selecting your core keywords. These form the cornerstone for your searches. They are the bricks or building blocks for your search strings.

One brick alone can't make a building. Together bricks can form many structures.

Your search objective statement will guide you in identifying the right focus for your keywords. It will also help define the words that will extract the right results from your database.

This may sound crazy but...

To add power to your search strings you need to get away from focusing on keywords that most accurately describe the skills you need to find. This is NOT what you need.

You did read that correctly. You DO NOT need keywords that define the right skills.

<u>Instead you need the keywords that return the most relevant and accurate results.</u>

That is a very critical distinction. A good keyword that defined the skills correctly but pulls many irrelevant or unwanted results is of no help.

Step 3: Developing Supporting Keywords

Even keywords that define a skill correctly can bring bad results. Discovering keywords that attract the same results through different expressions is critical.

Choosing supporting keywords is about translating a concept, not about defining the skills of the job.

Seems odd, doesn't it?

See, an individual keyword can be dragged down by being popularly used.

They get bloated with related words that the search engine things are helpful. The more popularly used word the more unwanted concepts that it will pull in that out rank the ones that you need.

Finding supporting keywords is about giving you the clearest advantages of by finding words that amplify the meaning of your core concept.

In other words, finding words that are going to have less scoring, which makes them provide better results.

Drilling down to specific keywords to gain greater control over the search results that are returned may appear difficult but it isn't.

Step 4: Upping your game with Concept Stemming!

Stemming takes the core keywords and finds those other keywords or concepts stemming from those ideas.

Recruiters will usually set aside keywords because they didn't experience relevant results. That is understandable but if they would have just researched to see which keywords branch out from those words they would have reaped the benefits that they were after.

Stem words are keywords that are often underutilized by other Recruiters, yet frequently used by prospective candidates. This makes them an excellent resource.

It's not challenging to find a random keyword, but it's tremendously difficult to narrow in on the spectacular ones.

The selection of specific and unique terms and adding appropriate context terms gives your search strings power.

Taking the time to do it will help you find the most relevant and accurate keywords. It will also give you the added bonus of helping you discover how they will work best together.

Step 5: Creating Word Images

All words can change their meaning by how we use them. Each word comes with a framework of associated concepts that cause the word to change with context.

By adding other words into our search we affect what the first one means, which in turn affects what, your database or search engine returns.

In other words, by adding keywords we can connect meanings to form associations that direct the context and direction of our search.

This word association enhances the meaning and strengthens relevancy scores. It also prevents algorithms from attracting irrelevant results.

<u>This makes associations created by linking keywords far more important to strong queries and to keyword performance than the meaning of the actual word itself.</u>

By placing keywords randomly together their association may be creating the wrong word image.

There's no question that the association of keywords is one of the best and easiest changes you can make to create the most meaningful impact on your search results.

Step 6: Integrating Your Keywords

The position of your keywords within a search string plays a pivotal role in search results.

Just from changing the sequential order of the keywords we are able to affect a tremendous change in the search results.

By a simple change in word location you can:

- Establish and change meaning
- Create new definitions as you see fit
- Control relevance scores.

The position of the keyword that you use is a key part of great search string design.

Hopefully, you abandoned the idea of just finding the word that defines your skills best.

You now need to think about concepts that truly addresses specific search needs. Does your choice communicate relevance to a specific need?

Much of finding great results involves other things such as relevance ranking scores, keyword density, proximity and perhaps some weight related to association.

It boils down to creating word positioning that does more than define a sought after skill.

Step 7: Taking Charge of your Search Strings

Until you run your search string in a database or search engine, the strategy needed to achieve the right results won't be revealed.

When you first run your search string, some elements come into play, which can modify the results. Some narrow your results too much, others not enough, while others may skew the direction of your search altogether.

<u>Strong choice of words, and clever positioning can't predict whether you will achieve the desired results from your search string.</u>

By understanding the chaos that is the search results, you can pinpoint the underlying causes of search string problems. Addressing the issue of irrelevant results is a matter of understanding what the search engine surmised your search intentions to be.

Effective search strings integrate address the real problems encountered as you search.

The many problems that Recruiters face in search string writing can be reduce to one.

Not clearly understanding what they are trying to accomplish with the query.

Step 8: Wiping out Irrelevant Results

As candidate profiles begin to come back from your search strings, the real query performance trends emerge. You may find specific words within your queries that are generating poor results.

Sometimes, even if you do everything right, search engines can still return irrelevant results. All it takes is one very popular keyword that pulls irrelevant and/or unwanted pages. The point is, bad results can happen even with good keywords.

Through the proper use of exclusions you can add the finishing touches to your already powerful statements to deliver the right message to your database.

Knowing how exclusions work and affect your search is key to taking full advantage of them and reducing search time. They can increase your ability to overcome the limitations of your queries.

If you don't select the exclusion or tell your database or search engine how you will be utilizing them, you might not get the results you are expecting. You could also lose relevant results.

These are the eight steps to creating super search strings. The system has worked for me throughout the years. The important thing is to start.

It might seem intimidating; to put it all together, but it is not. Even if you do not already got some sourcing experience under your belt, following the steps will allow you to confidently write robust queries that deliver the right candidates.

You need to have the right system in place to make the most of your database or search engine searches.

Everything needs to fit together to provide you precision and control over your search results. This system is geared for that purpose.

Keywords

The First Pillar of Super Search Strings Crafting

Chapter Two

Creating Your Search Objective

Step One: Creating A Search Objective

Writing powerful queries is kind of like making a cake.

A cake is not altogether that difficult to make but it requires following some methodical steps in a certain order.

If you were to place all the ingredients to make a cake on a table and then you told a child to go ahead and make a cake. Without any other instructions, it would be very unlikely that the child would be able to make a cake.

More than likely he would just make a mess.

A query is the equivalent to the cake instructions. The child is the database, and keywords and operators are the ingredients.

The database, like the child in the cake analogy, has no clue how to turn your keywords into relevant results. Given to its algorithms, the database just runs the keywords together and spits out whatever happens to be around.

Writing effective search strings is like writing a cake recipe. It involves tests, trial and failure, improvement, breakthroughs, and learning.

Just combining words at random and running search strings is not very effective.

Guiding your search results.

Writing super search strings is about doing more with less. With a very minimal number of keywords, you need to come up with an awesome resume for top qualified individuals.

The challenge of designing and implementing such a search string can be daunting.

- The different jobs to search on require different strategies.

- Variations in keyword meanings can lead to different results or limit the results within a search.

- Search engine algorithms can enhance or limit the flow of the much-needed results.

- Skills and knowledge change over time.

- No two people are exactly the same.

Recruiters who can navigate these variables and chart a route for their own search strategy will reach their goals faster and more efficiently than their competitors.

Knowing how to create and direct your search strings to deliver results is a strategic resource.

Creating great search strings is not about choosing great keywords.

Writing great queries isn't about identifying keywords so don't get hung up on them.

Many Recruiters get hung up on keywords without realizing that candidates can be found without using those cherished words. They believe that finding candidates is about finding those keywords mentioned in a page or profile; it is not.

Keywords have their place and we will get to that.

Great search strings don't just happen.

<u>Writing effective search strings is about delivering your search intentions effectively to the database, not listing keywords.</u>

The basis for a successful query is about setting the right expectations from the start.

Without setting the expectation, databases assumes that since the expectations are not clear any results will do.

Without defined expectations we would not be able to measure the effectiveness of our search string either.

Identifying a Search Objective

The way to develop the clear expectation for the search string is through the creation of a search objective.

So, what is a search objective?

It is a description of what you intend to achieve with your search strings.

It doesn't describe what they you will be doing, and it isn't a search string in and of itself. Instead it is a statement that "centers you."

It centers you on the skills, knowledge, and attributes that you will be attempting to produce through your search strings.

The search objective is a clear, precise statement of what your database should deliver. It is specific. It describes a context that defines the skills and attributes of your candidate. It forms the basis for the search approach and selection of tools.

For a database to deliver the right results it needs to be steered. Databases hang on your every word; they are ready to please you and to pounce on your every request. The database wants to give you the results you want but it can only respond to your instructions.

Defining the core concepts

The first step in creating our search objective is to review the job description and any related notes from conversations from stakeholders.

At first, our review of job description documentation should not focus on identifying keywords at all.

Resist the urge to start plugging keywords into your database. Instead focus on finding two or three primary ideas that represent the overall skills to be searched.

Many people are lucky enough to be able to find the right ideas to focus on without much difficulty. The reasons may vary, from having a thorough knowledge of the skills to be searched, to being intuitive, to somewhere in between.

Discovering the right ideas to focus your search with; may be a daunting task for others, however. This is especially so for those who happen to be working on a role that is new to them.

As we review job descriptions, there are some clues placed within them that are helpful as you consider your search.

Although the description may have many bullet points to describe the skills important to the role, those bullet points are often not useful for the purposes of your search.

The purpose in reviewing the job description is to select the ideas that best define the principal concepts to the search. The best bullets points are the ones that focus on one of three things.

The three things are: Performance, Conditions, or Criteria required for the job.

Performance
Performance related job requirements make good choices because they are simply description of the behavior that prospective candidates are expected to perform. These requirements describe what he will be doing.

For example:

- Be able to program in Java.
- Be able to design mobile application.
- Be able to design web pages.

In each of these instances you can tell the task that they will be performing. In these statements the key terms are program and / or design.

Here are a couple of poor of performance objectives examples:

- Sets and achieves build schedule
- Eliminates impediments

- Independently set tasks and complete work with limited direction.

These kinds of requirements are too vague and don't really describe anything useful to us.

Conditions
Another type of job requirements that are useful to us, come in the shape of conditional requirements. These set conditions that are a description of the circumstances under which the performance will be carried out. These conditions can help to prevent misunderstanding of the intent.

For example:

What will the candidates be expected to use when performing (e.g., tools, languages, operating systems, etc.)?

Here is an example of objectives with conditions:

- Formulate/define specifications for complex operating software-programming applications using engineering releases and utilities from programs.

- 4+ years of experience with Java programming (Android J2ME, or other small-footprint Java) -OR-

- 4+ years of experience with Objective C (iPhone)

In these descriptions, the need to use engineering releases and utilities programs, either that or the programming experience is conditional to specific languages, i.e. Java, Objective-C.

The clues here are the use of the words "using" and "with." The statements after those words are indicating the tools needed for the job.

Criteria
The third type of requirement or bullet point to look for are the ones focused on providing criteria.

The criterion is a description for acceptance of a performance as sufficient. In other words, how well must it be done?

Stating those things that let us know how well the candidates will have to perform to be considered competent. It also provides a standard against which to test the success of the search string, and gives you a way of evaluating whether the candidate is a match.

The criterion is sometimes specified in job descriptions as the necessarily minimum level. Here's an example of an objective with criteria:

- The developer will lead the entire app life cycle from concept until delivery and post launch support.

- Independently set tasks and complete work with limited direction

How do we use these statements?

When given the job descriptions to work on, they can be overwhelming. When selecting which job requirements are needed as the focus of our search objective, limit yourself to these three types of statements.

Let's try selecting three concepts to create our search objective.

A sample job description

Let's review a random job description for an iPhone developer as an example. The following job description is representative of many open requisitions today.

This should give us a good playground to learn.

> ... is in search of a senior mobile app developer to lead the design, development and maintenance of its iPhone applications. The developer will lead the entire app life cycle from concept until delivery and post launch support. In addition to delivering the product the successful candidate will be heavily involved in driving the mobile strategy but also will be

responsible for setting up, and maintaining the hardware and software that support the mobile apps.
Required Skills
* Sets and achieves build schedule
* Eliminates impediments
* Performs design reviews
* Performs code reviews
* Designs software using in OOA/D, UML, design patterns, data modeling, and ERDs
* Independently set tasks and complete work with limited direction
* Feature lead on major components of application
* Profiles and tunes applications for CPU/memory use for application as whole
* Carries self well with written and verbal communications
* Ability to devise creative technical solutions that can scale
* Very strong debugging skills
Required Experience
* 4+ years of experience with Java programming (Android J2ME, or other small-footprint Java) -OR-
* 4+ years of experience with Objective C (iPhone)
* Bachelor's degree or equivalent

Reading a job description like this one can be incapacitating as they are overloaded with many technical terms. This one in particular is also confusing because of the way it was written.

It has a job description, a required skills section, and a required experience section. All sections describe important functions of the role and it would be difficult to select keywords that are unique enough to get results.

If we were to ask a room full of Recruiters what three statements are the principal ones, we would get different answers. That is because there is no right or wrong.

There are quite a few words we can chose from within each of the sections.

As you begin, realize that it's okay not to know what the important ideas are. We all go through moments where we are just not sure and we reshuffle our thought processes. For now, you still shouldn't be concerned with which keywords are better, nor about how to find your candidate yet. That comes later.

Our clues for our first concept

Aim at pegging down the principal focus of the job. Returning to our "iPhone developer" job description, the job title will guide our keyword choices. As we read the list of keywords we need to ask: Which of these words specifies skills particularly related to iPhones?

What your focus should be in identify a keyword, or phrase, or short statement, which condenses the primary focus into a searchable concept.

You are seeking two or three concepts that, when combined, express your search goal.

In the very first sentence of the job description: "in search of a senior mobile app developer to lead the design." Even though this job description was titled "iPhone Developer," the initial line calls for someone with "mobile" experience.

This thought is reinforced with a couple of bullet points as follows:

* 4+ years of experience with Java programming (Android J2ME, or other small-footprint Java) -or-
* 4+ years of experience with Objective C (iPhone)

The requirements state that the focus of skills has to be Mobile and it could be represented in either Android based or iPhone based platforms. This makes Mobile a good choice for our primary focus.

This may seem a simple play on semantics but it is important. The programming languages are important but only as secondary concepts.

Here are some questions to guide your thought processes:

> What is the main skill that these candidate needs to possess?
> What most constitutes the focus of his work?
> What do they have to accomplish?
> What do they must possess?

Be sure to check your job description and see what concepts seem to be emphasized or repeated often.

Ask your self, "whenever a stakeholder or hiring manager reviews a resume, what skill needs to pop out at them as "the right one?"

Clues for our second concept

As we reviewed the types of bullets/job requirements, we mentioned that these last two bullet points were conditional. They both describe programming experience but it could be either J2ME OR Objective-C.

These describe our second concept that we can focus on.

Don't be tempted to go directly to the types of programming; the important idea here is the "programming experience."

The experience can be in either J2ME or Objective-C but there are others too i.e. small footprint Java. Because of that the bullet can be summarized then as requiring experience-programming applications."

Clues for our third concept

For the third core concept: There are so many other words that we can use that are written into the job description such as: "Sets and achieves build schedule." We can eliminate those because they don't help define the search.

The third core concept, it is a little trickier.

There are so many other words that we can use that are written into the job description such as: "Sets and achieves build schedule." We can eliminate those because they don't help define the search.

One of the bullet points does look promising:

> Designs software using in OOA/D, UML, design patterns, data modeling, and ERDs

This one is a strong candidate because it describes the different methodologies that the candidate will need. These are all skills such as OOA/D, UML, "design patterns," "data modeling," and ERD's that are needed for the design of the mobile applications.

Don't worry at this time whether you know what any of those acronyms mean.

The important thing to know here is that the one idea being described with them is that of design. This expresses the third concept needed for our search clearly.

It is imperative for you to go through the exercise of finding and selecting the key concepts that comprise your search objective.

The three concepts

We have now identified three concepts to pursue. So here are our three chosen concepts:

"Mobile"

"Applications"

"Design"

As we review these concepts, they seem reasonable because it stands to reason that these candidates will need to use the programming languages to design mobile applications.

They clearly summarize the position requirements. These concepts are the main ideas that our search strings need to convey regardless of what keywords we use. This is the most critical concept to the foundation of your search strings.

A good search objective is one that succeeds in communicating an intended result to the database. It is useful if it conveys to the database a picture of what a successful candidate will be able to do.

Points to Keep in Mind

In selecting a search objective we are making a conscious decision to focus on these concepts at the exclusion of all others.

This is so that we can keep a clear picture of what we need to find. From this point forward, until you finish this search this concepts will be the parameters that hold your search strings together.

Now that we selected these concepts as a search objective, clear the others from your mind. Ignore any keywords that do not relate to your search objective.

If the keywords that you are considering don't address one of the key concepts of your objective, is not a fit. Set it aside. If you were to use it, it would only serve to confuse your database.

That is why it is critical that the search objectives describe the intended results. To be useful to you they need to be specific so that they will help you to make sound keyword decisions later in the query writing process.

If you want to craft super queries, you need to have clearly defined concepts to target.

These key concepts will center your queries.

Summing up Search Objectives

The foundation is the most important part of any building. It is as important to your search strategy as well.

Defining you search objective is not about the selection of keywords.

The search objective is about creating a distinction of what precisely your query needs to achieve before starting to run queries.

Once the search objective is defined it makes it easy to isolate specific meanings or context to increase the precision of your search strings.

A search objective will also make it easier to seek out those keywords best equipped, because of their definition and related concepts, to define our search targets. It will provide the means to combine them in strategic ways with the Boolean operators to provide specific messages.

Establishing the objective will help you gain your control, deliver precision, and to get results coming back timely.

The power of the search objective is in its ability to create or craft out your a message in a way which your database will understand. It creates search strings that educate and control your database.

Through it, your queries will command your database to follow your instructions and to bring back exactly what you need.

It is important to begin with determining the search objectives, and then decide on the most effective keywords, NOT the other way around.

After generating the search objective, you will be ready to move to next steps of the search string design process, including the identification and selection of keywords and operators.

Keyword Research

The Second Pillar of Super Search Strings

Chapter Three

The Secret to Selecting Highly Effective Keywords

Step Two – Selecting Core Keywords

We all want to find the magical keyword. We want candidates to sweep down onto our databases like hordes of starving locusts. We want qualified candidates applying to our open roles.

But wishing won't get us anywhere.

Yes, when it's just you and database, you have work to do.

You need to find keywords that bring results.

Choosing the best keywords for your search string is an art, blended with a bit of science.

Keywords seduce most of us. I know they certainly seduced me. For years I've been paying attention to the things that affect keywords, both in databases and search engines, and made note of the techniques that work.

The words that you seek are sitting there in the search objective you just have to know what to do with them.

Precision will come from making right keyword choices. Those choices can develop from only one thing; proper research which is based on your search objective.

Core Keywords

Let's walk through a simple example that explains how we can conduct our own core keyword selection.

Our search objective gave us the initial keywords, mobile platforms, application programming experience, and design methodologies.

We will use a spreadsheet to help us organize the results of our research. You can use whatever works for you — spreadsheet, Word document, or regular physical notebook or journal.

Concept One Mobile	Concept Two Application programming	Concept Three Design

This will help us how to organize and categorize our words.

Now we are ready to move on to the next step, determining whether our possible keywords are a good fit for our search strategy.

Identifying your Core keywords

We can see that from the initial description that there are two mobile platforms mentioned directly. We know that the skills would be represented in either "mobile," "Android," or "iPhone."

We'll dump those into what I'll call our core keyword bucket.

So our core keywords for mobile platforms could look like this:

Mobile platforms

- Mobile
- Android
- IPhone

For now we shouldn't be concerned with the fact that they are generic keyword are broad in their definition.

In the upcoming steps this keywords will transform for now these are only concerned with selecting our core keywords. Core keywords are those that directly describe the skill set that you are searching for.

Notice how closely the keywords are tied to our intended meaning?

That seems easy enough, right?

We can break down our second core concept in much the same way. For that we will use the concept of application programming. In the description we are given some keyword for that already. These give us a quick way to find our core keywords.

Application programming

- Java
- J2ME
- Small footprint Java
- Objective-C

Repeating the process one more time as we do the same thing to the third core concept of application programming. In the definition we are given some keyword for that already. These give us a quick way to find our core keywords.

Design Methodologies

- UML
- OOA/OOD
- Data Modeling
- ERD's

Categorizing and organizing keywords in this way will be useful when it comes to building your search strings.

What to do with these keywords

Notice that you haven't written any search strings yet at this point ... you've just built three buckets of keywords.

Concept One Mobile platforms	Concept two Application Programming	Concept two Application Programming
mobile	Java	UML
iPhone	J2ME	OOA/OOD
Android	Small Footprint java	Data modeling
	Objective-C	ERD's

By incorporating your concepts into a table, you can create a visual image of how your keywords may overlap.

Keep in mind: the keywords within each column will have to avoid duplicate concept issues, and to work well for the definition of your core concepts, which are always your primary focus.

We could easily use the table to start creating some good search strings.

We could combine the keywords, using one from each column and it would express our search intent clearly. Let's try some quick queries:

(Mobile AND J2ME AND UML)
(Android AND "Java ME" AND OOD)
(iPhone AND Objective-C AND ERD's)

Granted these search strings are not very effective but they already convey the basic message of our search objective.

The intent in going through this exercise is not to get you to use these for search strings yet.

This compiled list is met to be the words that will help us uncover our target keywords.

Through the next steps we will elaborate on these to find our supporting and stemming keywords that will be form a strategic part of our search sting.

There are countless words out there that are calling to be used in the building our search string. This list will focus our choices.

Wild goose chase proofing your search strings

As you compile your own table, make sure that the core keywords you are considering are highly relevant to your ultimate goal.

Creating the list is an important step to "wild-goose chase" proofing your search.

<u>Keywords are the bricks or building blocks for your search strings. One brick alone can't make a building. Together bricks can form many structures.</u>

Choosing core concepts sets up a search right from the start, while helping you build search results that lead to great candidate profiles.

The idea is that this list will be a work in progress, a list that you will add to as you do your research and find other words.

Consider this list as your keyword power center.

The keyword power center is where you will draw your concepts from, and where you will keep returning to as you get stuck. It will become essential as you experience difficulties.

It's become a non-negotiable element of my search string process, and I hope it becomes the same for you.

Crafting search strings is hard work. It's not hard like designing a space ship. It is more a like working on your taxes kind of hard.

By applying these elements to your own queries you will improve your chances for a good results. You will also be making your search string crafting process a whole lot easier.

We are not done yet...

The next step of the search string design process will have us developing supporting keywords.

Supporting keywords will:

1. Expand the reach of your queries
2. Create keyword images
3. Provide more search string precision

In the next chapter, you will also learn how to create a system for keyword research to maximize your keywords.

Chapter Four

Keywords with a Supporting Role

Step Three – Finding the Right "Supporting" Keywords

You've work hard to find the right word, you interview stakeholders, you read technical definitions, choose each word carefully. You finally hit "send," and what happens?

They didn't find anything. They were just duds! Not even one decent prospect.

What do you do? Do you go back and spend hours looking for new words? Do you just give up on your database and hit the phones?

The answer may be easier than you might expect.

Two words: Supporting keywords

Supporting keywords are the easiest way to fine-tune your keywords.

What are Supporting Keywords?

Supporting Keywords are the words that are developed from your core concepts that are synonymous or closely related concepts.

Finding supporting keyword can help you find less commonly used word that convey the same message and expand your results.

Supporting words are ...

Even if you are already be familiar with the skill set that you are searching for, take the time to research your core keywords.

Even keywords that define a skill correctly can bring bad results.

Discovering other keywords that attract the same results through different expressions is important.

Generally, any single core term can have many supporting words or phrases. Supporting keywords will provide overlapping coverage over meaning.

These overlaps would allow you to exercise better control through your search strings.

A good place for us to begin is Wikipedia, where we will look up the keyword J2ME.

Wikipedia makes keyword research simple, efficient, and completely painless. Instead of using multiple sites to conduct our research, we have got one easy-to-use tool that will give us much of the information we need.

As you read the description keep an eye out for synonymous concepts to the keywords "J2ME."

Look for suggested keywords; pick a few to dig into further.

A small cut out has been included below for your review:

> Java Platform, Micro Edition
> From Wikipedia, the free encyclopedia
> (Redirected from J2ME)
> Java Platform, Micro Edition, or Java ME, is a Java platform designed for embedded systems (mobile devices are one kind of such systems). Target devices range from industrial controls to mobile phones (especially feature phones) and set-top boxes. Java ME was formerly known as Java 2 Platform, Micro Edition (J2ME). Originally developed under the Java Community Process as JSR 68, the different flavors of Java ME have evolved in separate JSRs.

On reading the description on Wikipedia, we find several words that can be used as supporting keyword. These words are synonymous to J2ME.

These words or phrases are:

1. "Java 2 platform, Micro Edition."
2. "Java ME"
3. JME
4. Java Platform, Micro Edition.

Notice how closely the keyword phrases are tied to our intended meaning?

This means that they're typical words that are exchangeable for the acronym J2ME.

This makes them keywords that we can use. For now, we can add them to our Power Keyword Center table:

Concept two Application Programming
Java
J2ME
JME
"Java ME"
"Java 2 platform, Micro Edition"
"Java Platform, Micro Edition"

Do you see the different ways the same concept can be expressed? This process offers us different supporting keywords that express the same skill set. These offer us other possible terms to search by that may not be so widely used, making them better acronyms.

You may think; this is too easy. It is!

Databases don't define your words

Returning to our bullet points, we can pick up another keyword to research further. We will try our trusty Wikipedia for Objective C:

> "Objective-C is a general-purpose, high-level, object-oriented programming language that adds Smalltalk-style messaging to the C programming language. It is the main programming language used by Apple for the OS X and iOS operating systems and their respective APIs, Cocoa and Cocoa Touch."

This definition tells us that Objective-C is the main programming language for the Apple iOS and OS X and their APIs, Cocoa and Cocoa Touch.

These keywords give us other alternative keywords that we can use to search on that can each gives us another form to find the equivalent skill sets.

This brief description describes several words that can serve well as supporting keywords. These words or phrases are:

1. iOS
2. OS X
3. Cocoa
4. Cocoa Touch

Notice how closely the keyword phrases are tied to our intended meaning? This means may not mean the same as our keywords but they are closely tied to it.

Even though these words aren't strictly synonymous. All of which require "Objective C." Because of their relationship to Objective-C they will create the right context that we need.

Concept two Application Programming
Java
J2ME
JME
"Java ME"
"Java 2 platform, Micro Edition"
"Java Platform, Micro Edition"
Objective-C
iOS
OSX

This simple research technique has tremendous potential to enhance the results of your search strings.

Databases and search engines are not humans; they are programs that match your selected keyword to words found on the candidates' profiles.

It may surprise you to know that databases and search engines don't define words.

They don't look for synonyms either.

That is totally up to you. If you don't do it, the database doesn't care.

Each of the variations of your core concepts can help you expand your search results.

<u>In particular, you have to understand that you're translating a concept, not an individual word.</u>

As you consider which keywords to use, look for words that are complementary to your core concepts. It doesn't matter which keyword or term you are using, there are always alternative ways to express it.

Following this process will help you find elegant ways to expand your search into more accurate candidate profiles.

There is another concept in our original search objective statement to expand on as well. That is that of the design skills.

The original descriptions had listed them as UML, OOA, OOD, etc....

We could approach this concept by looking for synonymous ways to describe OOD, which might include "object oriented design," or OOP, or "object oriented programming," "object oriented analysis," and "object oriented design," among others.

Drilling down to more specific keywords to gain greater control over the search results that are returned may appear difficult but it isn't.

As you research your keywords your goal is to identify any word ambiguity and to translate selected concepts to other searchable terms to expand your word base.

One of the best tools we have is that of specificity, which means the exactness or the narrowness with which a keyword or term you select describes the candidate skill that you are looking for.

Specificity does not refer to how the database deals with keywords but rather your selection of words themselves.

Specificity

Specificity can help you focus your search string in with laser precision or zoom out to widen your net.

As a means of a simple clarification let's consider the word "Cat" as a keyword for instance.

There would be several ways that we could use to look up the concept of cat. We could use words like "feline," "house cat," "domestic cat," or even "felis catus" which is the scientific classification.

We might decide to go the route of breed names such as Burmese, Sphinx, or Siamese. "Siamese" is more specific than "cat," which is itself more specific than "feline."

Foundational concept: One of the clearest advantages of seeking the most specific keywords is that you gain insight into other words that can help you locate a very specific reference, even if it is only mentioned a single time in the database.

The goal is to not miss any high potential keywords.

Just note that the more unusual the term the more specific results you will achieve.

In other words, the more rare the term the more likely it is to lower the number of results from your search string.

Use your core keywords to build a list of the skills, acronyms and searchable concepts.

Try to include as many of them as you can find. Be indiscriminate in your choices, this is especially important. Don't discriminate on words because they describe the skill set weakly or are too generic.

Chapter Five

Not Your Traditional Stemming

Step Four – Strengthening Queries thru Stemming

When it comes down to keyword research, using keyword-stemming methods to find variants is an amazing strategy.

It is a simple technique of generating several new words from a single keyword.

It is an effective way to generate more hits from the search your search strings. It is also effective at increasing the accuracy of same results.

What is this amazing tool?

It is called; Keyword stemming, and it is used for extending the reach of a targeted keyword.

The stemming refers to the growth of one keyword or phrase that is related to your search. Stemming is a way of making one keyword or phrase into many additional new words.

While supporting words dealt with finding synonymous concepts, stemming focuses on growing your words. Think of it like a flower stemming into many branches.

It makes sense to expand the scope of your keywords, doesn't it?

Harnessing the Power of your Keywords thru Stemming!

Example of concept stemming:

The mobile concept that we started gave us two already defined concepts those were that of Android and iPhone OS.

These are operating systems. If we did a quick search to define Mobile Operating systems, we would find a list that would include these others popular mobile platforms.

- Palm OS
- webOS
- BlackBerry
- Windows Mobile
- Symbian

I didn't include a full list of other popular mobile platforms but are they useful? Darn skippy, they are.

All of the keywords are distinctly related to ur search. Not only do they data allow him to narrow our focus, but it shows us other keywords to explore.

These all express mobile platforms and all stem from our initial concept. They are concepts that are used for the same purpose. They stem from the same concept.

An example of "Stemming" keywords

Now it's time to step into our keyword research mode.

Stemming makes sense.

It is a good method to expand your main keyword or phrase into a number of variable options.

For an example let's look deeper into the Android J2ME environments.

In Wikipedia again, we can look at the Android Operating system a little closer. Android has seen numerous updates, adding new features and fixing bugs.

Each major release is named in alphabetical order after a dessert or sugary treat. Some of these are listed here:

Cupcake = version 1.5
Donut = version 1.6
KitKat = version 4.4.2.

We could list those as other stemming concepts. These would make great stemming words, as they are specific to work done using J2ME. These keywords build a larger picture behind "J2ME."

Isn't it easy!

How do we use concept stems?

It isn't difficult to find stemming concepts. The key takeaway is: research your keywords and keep an open mind as you see the definitions and related concepts.

Through them you can create easy search strings like:

> Android (J2ME AND (Cupcake OR Donut OR KitKat) AND UML

Key Observation: Notice in the search string above how the keywords Cupcake, Donut, KitKat, alone would not be good search words for us. But used strategically with our core keywords they contribute to better results.

These keywords stemming from our core keywords helped us write a more specific search string that will pull candidates that others are missing out on.

Again as a side note, this query is not ready for searching. The purpose in using it here was to show you how it will combine with our supporting keywords to create better search strings. We will review how to turn your keywords into queries soon.

Hang in there!

Research your keywords

Often stemming keywords may carry less significance than the core keywords themselves.

Just searching for cupcake alone would take us away from our search goal but combined with our core keywords it changed meaning and amplified context.

Because a word sounds generic doesn't mean that it is any less valuable.

It just means that you should not substitute your keywords for their variants, but use these keyword variations along with the keyword.

Use our example as a guide.

As Recruiters, many of us think of keyword research as something that we have to force ourselves to do.

Keyword research is:

Dull
Mundane
Tedious
Bland
Banal

I'm sure you can find other appropriate words to describe it.

Research is hard

Keyword research isn't stimulating, intriguing, or fun. (Unless you are like me, than you might find it fun!)

Keyword research isn't as glamorous as the actual work of interviewing candidates, sending out offer letters, and on-boarding hires.

Keyword research is hard because you have to wade through massive amounts of irrelevant keywords to get to the useful nuggets that help you find your target.

Sifting through all those words is tiresome. There is not much difficulty in going to Wikipedia and looking up your keywords. The difficulty is in keeping your eyes from glossing over as you read.

I get it!

In spite of that, researching which keywords to use and which are not effective is one of the most important activities you'll do as a Recruiter.

It is specifically because it's hard that it's one of the best things for us to do. Because it's difficult, it's likely that other Recruiters aren't doing it.

The Importance of Keyword Research

Stemming will help you build a comprehensive listing of targeted keywords or phrases that cover a spectrum of thematically associated subjects.

It will reveal those relevant keywords that are not being used or are used less by other Recruiters, yet frequently used by prospective candidates.

It's worth a second mention that having a greater variety of keywords through stemming can help you express your words in ways candidates may be doing.

<u>The usefulness of keyword research cannot be overstated.</u>

Taking the time to do it will help you find the most relevant and accurate keywords. It will also give you the added bonus of helping you discover how they will work best together.

Researching your keywords will improve your search results dramatically.

The selection of specific and unique terms and adding appropriate context terms gives your search strings power.

Awaken your keyword Hunter

No doubt there's a creative keyword Hunter spirit inside you! It just needs waiting to be released.

The best keywords are hiding. They need a hunter to sniff them out and pounce on them.

Get excited over hunting for new keywords.

Look for keywords that trigger stellar results.

<u>It's not challenging to find a random keyword, but it's tremendously difficult and satisfying to narrow in on the spectacular ones.</u>

Breakthroughs in keyword hunting require a blend of an intimate knowledge of the keywords being searched and the subtle ways that keywords work.

- Research the different keyword influences for each of your keywords.
- Dig a bit deeper into related words and phrases.
- Determine the usefulness of each of your core keywords
- The trick is to have the right definition of your keywords from the start.

This is critical to good keyword hunting.

Summing up Stems

If research great keywords automatically led to great results, things would be different.

Of course we know that there's more to it than that. That is because we are not just looking for keywords we are looking for people. Your keywords need to be put into a context that pulls prospective candidates.

It helps to have a focus as we perform our keyword research.

Focus on...

Focus your search on words that are underutilized by other Recruiters, yet frequently used by prospective candidates.

Focus on finding keywords, which will not just define but expand those core concepts.

Focus on words that provide the best control over the elements and algorithms.

Many Recruiters resort to using keywords as found in the job description or as given by stakeholders / hiring managers. This has become the "go to" or default practice for them, as at first glance it appears to work.

They do find some candidates, which mention those keywords. Usually though, the mention of those is not enough.

Searching with those keywords will inevitably end with frustration by a lack of qualified candidates. That may be the reason you are reading this book!

Don't get stuck using those keywords!

The apparent results found from them can keep you from finding better performing ones. They can also lead you to many hours of wasted time and effort and often derail your overall sourcing strategy.

The notion that keywords found in the job description or given to us by hiring managers are the right ones is a fallacy.

Hiring managers know about the job.

They don't know how to search.

To achieve the type of results reserved for top performers, you have to stretch yourself beyond your limits and undertake keyword research.

In doing so you will learn to target your prospective candidate as a whole.

That is by far the most important aspect in any candidate search initiative. It is the process of aiming at the right candidates.

Integration of Keywords
....
The Third Pillar of Super Search Strings

Chapter Six

Creating Word Images

Step Five – The Power of putting keywords together

For writers or novelists, using a language that vividly paints a picture for their readers is a necessity.

They have to write word images that lure their readers and make them want to read more. This ability to paint a word picture is useful in different professional areas such as sales, creative writing and speeches or presentations.

It is even applicable to writing queries.

The application might not be that obvious, considering that databases can't understand the meaning of words, can't understand sarcasm, or wit, and can't infer ideas from our words

<u>Why would use vivid language for such a database?</u>

We do it not because we were trying to describe a skill set.

We would do so for the same reason writers do it.

They use words to paint vivid pictures to evoke a response from their readers. We use keywords because by using them we want to elicit a response from the database.

Evoking a response

Imagine searching for the keyword JAVA.

Do you mean the island of Java, the coffee, or the programming language?

Before anyone, including your database, could understand what you need, there would need to be other words in the query to make your intent clear.

The way keywords are used and understood often boils down to a difference in the way the words are being interpreted. Also, all words can change the meaning by how we use them.

In other words, the meaning of a word isn't all that important.

We make natural associations of ideas to words.

Each word comes with a framework of associated concepts that cause the word to change with context.

If we wanted to drive our search for "Java" as a keyword towards the programming language, we would combine it with other technical terms such as XML and JSP, which would establish the meaning of Java as a programming language.

If we would rather search for information on the Island of Java, we might combine it with keywords like "population density," "history," or "demographics."

A word by itself may not mean much but in association with others it may turn into gold.

As you can see, keywords are important. We need them to search with, but it isn't the words that matters so much as <u>the image that they paint.</u>

What matters more is how the different words combine to create a context or to change relevancy.

This word association enhances the meaning.

Through the associations made with other keywords every, each word has the potential to not only to change the meaning, but to bring about totally different results.

<u>Foundational concept: The combination of the keywords changes the context of the search string.</u>

This makes associations created by linking keywords far more important to strong queries and to keyword performance than the meaning of the actual word itself.

Grouping our keywords

Databases draw meaning from associating keywords with other words.

Since keywords build context together, it makes since to group them together.

Writing a search string with a list of random keywords is not the idea. Just putting them words together for the sake of putting them together doesn't work.

By the way, that is what many Recruiters do in their search strings and all they have to show for it is frustration.

Before I show you the way to group words together let's discuss what grouping keywords accomplishes.

Grouping words does four things:

1. It focuses your keywords into ideas or concepts.
2. It tells the database that the words are related.
3. It will expand the power of the keywords to cover more search possibilities.
4. It provides a method for controlling the meanings of statement.

An Example of Grouping

The goal is to group keywords to help the database understand and define our search concepts better.

Now we can look at how to group them together. Now we can start putting to use some of keywords that we have researched and gathered and organize into our table.

Concept One Mobile	Concept Two Application	Concept Three Design
Mobile	Android JAVA	UML
iPhone	J2ME	OOA
Android	Objective-C	OOD

The columns now make it easy to see that if we use the words in any one of the columns they will all be synonymous. Lets take the first concept of mobile and use it to write as a simple example:

(Mobile OR Android OR iPhone)

It seems simple and easy. Using the words that we already organize makes it easy to determine which words to use in a group.

Grouping Large Numbers of keywords

Let's use the second concept to create another simple grouping:

We could list them all as follows:

> (j2me OR "Java ME" OR JME OR
> "Java 2 platform, Micro Edition"
> OR "Java Platform, Micro Edition"
> OR "Objective C" OR iOS OR OSX
> OR COCOA OR "COCOA Touch")

There is no set total number of keywords that you can use in a search string. This would unlikely be too confusing for a database.

Think in terms of three when grouping your keywords, and you'll likely end up with a more engaging search strings.

> (j2me OR "Java ME" OR JME)

The in the idea of the J2ME programming language experience through our research we have expanded to include a few more keywords and phrases.

There is however; a limit to the number of total words you can use in a search string altogether. Most database will limit you to about sixteen (16) keywords in total. Google let's you use about thirty-two (32).

Combining Groups

When you group similar keywords, you'll have a keyword dense statement, which will create a stronger context when you build your search string.

The power of the grouping of keywords is that it helps you organize and combine keyword concepts to form the desired level of meaning and context.

Let's blend these two groups of words.

(Mobile AND Android AND iPhone) AND (j2me OR "Java ME" OR JME)

As a form of explanation let's quickly review the use of parentheses here.

Notice that each statement is separated by parentheses.

Separating the words into groups sends a clearer message to your database.

By combining words into separate groups the database knows that it can use only those grouped together interchangeably.

The words enclosed are considered of equal value.

Merging Groups

Each parenthesis is read by the database separately and individually. After completing the instructions in each query, the database joins the results from each before showing you the results.

The combination of the two previous statements made a more complex search string but it is still not well defined.

To define our concept more clearly we would benefit from merging, rather than blending the two statements instead. Try this:

(Android AND (j2me OR "Java ME" OR JME))

This statement combines only the idea of Android with the J2ME grouping. Most of all because each concept is separated and grouped, it creates a context for the database to grab on to.

This statement tells the database; return either "Android J2ME" OR "Android Java ME" OR "Android JME."

Notice that in merging the two parentheses, we embedded one inside of the other. This technique of embedding parentheses is called nesting.

Complex Nesting

Parentheses nesting is used to provide more control by merging search strings to not only change the default order in which the keywords are processed, but to separate the order in which Boolean operators are processed as well.

Since our keywords come in two natural groupings, one for android and one of iPhone. Let's break them up into separate queries as follows.

(Android AND (j2me OR "Java ME" OR JME))

(IPhone AND ("Objective C" OR iOS OR OSX))

As you can see, these two statements were built the same way.

The difference between them is that one is focused on iPhone while the other focuses on Android. As far as our search objective is concerned these two statements are asking for the same skills set.

So rather than to used them both to combine separate instructions we can merge them:

((Android AND (j2me OR "Java ME" OR JME)) AND (iPhone AND ("Objective C" OR iOS OR OSX)))

This is already a really complex search string.

It has a total of five statements within parentheses.

Before going further we should test to make sure that the complex search string works and that we are on the right track.

You could enter this search string, in Google for instance, as it is to see how it works. To do that we will need to offer two tweaks just to highlight the need for resumes. Otherwise we would just get a bunch of articles.

The tweaks will include the addition of the keyword "resume" and the instruction; filetype:pdf.

These two refinements place a strong emphasize on resumes and should yield at least some good results.

The new search string would look as follows:

> **resume ((Android AND (j2me OR "Java ME" OR JME)) AND (iPhone AND ("Objective C" OR iOS OR OSX))) filetype:pdf**

As the following screen shot shows: the results are adobe acrobat's PDF format.

They are all resumes. The skills reflect mobile development in either iPhone or Android.

This search string seems to be targeting both iPhone developers' resumes well.

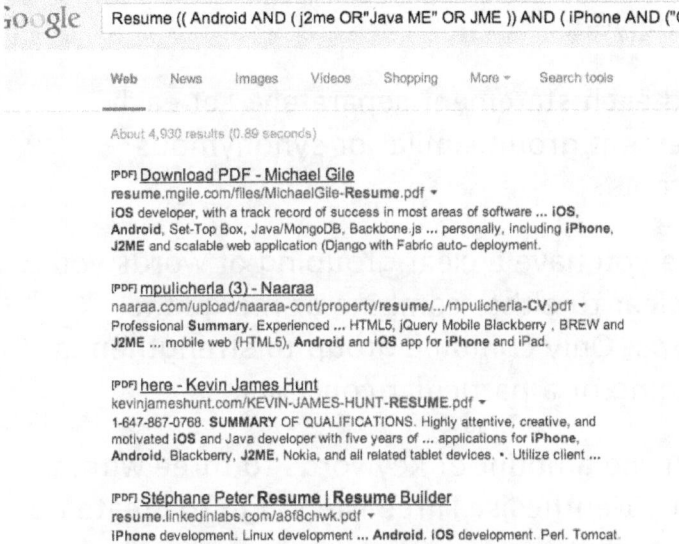

At this point it would be helpful to narrow the results to a geographical area. We will review how to do that closer detail in Chapter eight.

We are still not done.

There are a couple more steps in the process to make this a super search string.

Tips for building complex queries

Just grouping words together doesn't serve a purpose. You have to build and manage the instructions for your database.

That's easier said than done. Here are some tips to guide you:

- Build each statement separately. Let each statement group similar or synonymous concepts.

- Once you have a clear grouping of words you are clear to either combine or merge the groups. Only combine group to strengthen a meaning or a particular concepts.

- Limit the amount of keywords to three within each parenthesis. Three is enough to create a strong context.

- Once combined; watch the overall meaning of the statement. The more keywords or phrases that you use, the less each one will be emphasized.

By creating unique clusters, you create a level of focus that generates powerful ideas.

Let clusters or groupings lead you to breakthrough ideas.

Summing up Groups

Word associations are really powerful ways to create vivid word images for the databases. They allow us to define the framework of associated concepts the database should use.

Through the strategic grouping of keywords we gain the ability to establish meaning and definitions as we see fit to change the context of the search string.

Keywords are important but only in that we can create combinations to connect meanings that direct the context, direction, ranking, and relevance of our search.

Chapter Seven

Keyword Positioning

Step Six – Integrating words thru strategic positioning

Obviously, in an ideal world, you'll want the skills that you seek to appear first in the search results.

Achieving that however, requires finding the right balance between context and relevance scores of your keywords.

In this fight, the position of your keyword within your search string can be the difference between success and failure. In this chapter we will learn the reasons why the position of your keywords within a query is more important than the keywords themselves.

Search engines and databases attach importance to the sequence or order or position of your keywords.

They look at the position of your keyword in relation to other keywords, to the position of the word within a page, the position of words in titles and headers and others.

Every search string that you run is affected by the position of the keywords that you use. Databases and search engines use a fairly complex system to organize your results.

Why does the position of keywords matter?

Databases use a system called relevance ranking to calculate and display the results of your search.

This system arranges the results based on a measurement of likeness between your query and the content of each record.

This measurement is the calculation database of how the database understands what you need to see.

Having said that, it begs the question, how do databases determine what is relevant?

There is no scientific way to calculate relevancy, as it is an abstract thought and a very individual concept. That is because only you can tell what you needed.

<u>Databases can't tell want is relevant to you. Only you can say whether what you received is relevant to you or not.</u>

To a database relevance means more than finding a page with the right words. It is a way it tries to determine how well the pages that you see meet your needs. There are hundreds of factors that influence how database calculates relevance.

Relevance and your search strings

In essence relevance ranking is a calculation. Databases count the keywords and place a score on them. It then uses that score to assess the quality of the listed results. The higher the score the more relevant to you it is considered. The lower the score and it will be pushed down to the bottom of the list.

Let's try a sample search to get a point of reference. We will run the following query for JAVA programmers in Google as a baseline:

{ resume JAVA XML VB }

gle resume JAVA XML VB

Web   Images   Maps   Shopping   More ▾   Search tools

About 4,110,000 results (0.28 seconds)

Ad related to **resume JAVA XML VB** ⓘ
XML Resume Parsing - Certified HR-**XML Resume** Schema
www.sovren.com/
Open API, Open Standards. Demo Now!

XML Resumes | Tech Resumes | IT Resume Database | Dev Bistro
www.devbistro.com/resumes/keywords/XML ▾
XML Resumes posted daily on DevBistro.com. Search and ...

Notice that there are 4,100,000 results from this basic query.

As a comparison and to attempt to figure out what is happening, we will move the keyword Java to a different place within the search string, as displayed below:

{resume XML VB JAVA}

The total number of results decreased from 4.1 million on the last run to 2.79 million on this one.

That is a big difference especially since we used exactly the same keywords.

Their meaning didn't change, nor did their placement on the web pages themselves. The only thing that changed was the order in which we used them.

Just from changing the sequential order of the keywords we were able to affect a tremendous change in the ranking of the results.

What caused the change in results?

The query instructed the database that the primary intent is to find web pages that have the term "resume" in them and then they must have "Java" as a second priority and in a lesser priority the term "XML."

The database will give preference to those results that matched the request exactly as you entered first.

Through the reshuffling of the keywords two things happen.

1. First by changing keyword order you are changing the meaning of your keywords. This is because databases use a keywords association with other keywords to interpret meaning.

2. The order of keywords determines their relevance score. In other words, the sequence of the keywords denotes or designates their rank, priority or weight.

Search engines and databases alike will give priority to results that match not just the words but also the order in which you enter them.

Positioning Keywords

Just from changing the sequential order of the keywords we were able to affect a tremendous change in the ranking of the results.

The assumption is that your first keyword is the most important concept of your search.

Whichever word you enter into your search box first will affect your results more.

As a keyword is moved to a different place within the query it's overall ranking score will be affected.

To deemphasize a keyword just move it to a lesser position. On the other hand, to emphasize a keyword do the opposite and just move it closer to the front.

Through this simple exercise of positioning keywords within your search string we can change the meaning of your keywords.

This can also be a powerful tool to manipulate the relevance rankings to cause keywords to rise or fall in your results.

<u>This should highlight the importance choosing the right sequential order of keywords within your search strings.</u>

Bad Keyword Positioning

Let's try an example:

Let's suppose that our job descriptions calls for a programmer with JAVA skills. As we would continue reading our job description we would see that other technical skills include SOAP XML KERNELS.

Bad keyword positioning would look like this:

[resume JAVA Programmer SOAP XML Kernels]

You might think that you added many related words to create context for the database to understand what you need. In reality this query would be very confusing to your database.

What went wrong?

Where do we even begin?

Ignoring the fact that this search sting doesn't separate the words to create concepts. It's full of too many scattered keywords. They go all over the board in skills definition.

We said this before, but it bears repeating: The database cannot infer ideas from words. These search string does not create an image. Don't make the database try to figure out what you want. It can't figure it out.

Each word carries with it a connotation

The term JAVA associated with the keyword SOAP will create a context of JAVA designer or Architects. That is because SOAP deals with the access protocols and is used as part of Service Oriented Architecture.

The keyword JAVA paired with the term XML will return more web application developers. XML deals with the encoding of documents on the web.

The keyword JAVA paired with the keyword KERNELS will return more of a systems programmer, etc.

You can combine them in different ways to take you to different skill sets within the JAVA world but lumping them all together, your results will be loosely matched at best.

The search string needs to define the search concept clearly.

It needs to separate concepts. It needs to identify and position keywords in combinations to clearly direct the database.

When in doubt, follow a sample search string. Sometimes it can help to draw comparisons to other search strings.

Keyword Positioning in Action

To help you create a comparison, we will review an example of obvious positioning.

These are keywords that appear to go well together so they are used in a search string. Just because they are synonymous it doesn't mean that you should. They are only one step up from bad keyword positioning is choosing keyword order which is obvious and general.

Let's use the following query as a baseline for comparison. Resume JAVA Beans XML

Resume JAVA Beans XML

Web   Videos   Images   Shopping   News   More ▾   Sea

About 1,170,000 results (0.34 seconds)

Resume of Bear Bibeault
www.bibeault.org/ ▾
Technologies used include **Java**, **JavaBeans**, Java Servlets, JavaServer Pag 2.0), JSTL, EL, Ajax, HTML, DHTML, **XML**, JAXB, JAXP, **XML** Schema, ...

In this simple query, the keyword "resume" is the highest weighted word, "JAVA" is the second, while "Beans" ranks the third, which makes "XML" the least weighted word.

In comparison to the query below, JAVA, J2EE, and JME will now have been given the first place.

Resume (JAVA OR J2EE OR JME) Beans XML

Resume (JAVA OR J2EE OR JME) Beans XML

Web   Videos   Images   Shopping   News   More ▾   Search t

About 3,020,000 results (0.46 seconds)

Resume of Bear Bibeault
www.bibeault.org/ ▾
Technologies used include **Java**, **JavaBeans**, Java Servlets, JavaServer Pages (2.0), JSTL, EL, Ajax, HTML, DHTML, **XML**, JAXB, JAXP, **XML** Schema, ...

As you can see, the total number of keywords just about doubled with the introduction of the grouping.

Instead of refining the search string it amplified it.

Setting keywords off in parentheses changes the way search string is read by the database. Search engines / databases normally read keywords in your search strings from left to right.

In this instance, Java was overly emphasized. The search string manipulated the ranking algorithms to emphasize the importance of not only JAVA but also made its synonyms equal to it as well.

Clever of Positioning Keywords

You can take position to an even higher level than just emphasizing keywords:

(((Applications OR software) AND (Oracle OR Sybase)) AND (Engineer OR designer))

As you might have noticed, the parentheses caused the search engine to read inside out. This query asked the search engine to look for either Oracle or Sybase first. In order of the nested levels of keywords set off by the parentheses. The second instruction is to match those to either application or software.

Each keyword concept is confined by a separate set of parentheses. Each asks the database to return the phrases as results:

Oracle applications engineer	Sybase applications engineer
Oracle applications designer	Sybase applications designer
Oracle software engineer	Sybase software engineer
Oracle software designer	Sybase software designer

Another example of keyword positioning

One of the most important elements of an effective search string is keyword positioning.

Sensible and empirical positioning of keywords can make the difference between a successful search string strategy and a huge waste of time.

This is true regardless of whether you are using an Applicant tracking database, or a job board like CareerBuilder, or a search engine such as Google.

The results will be always be affected by the keyword order.

This next query is a type of search string that I see commonly used by Recruiters.

Resume ((Engineer OR designer) AND ((Oracle OR Sybase) AND (applications OR software)))

At first glance this query looks great. It has strategic selection of keywords. It has carefully adopted grouping through placement of parentheses.

That description makes the query sound perfect, so, what is wrong with it?

Here's the skinny

This search string is normally written to elicit resumes from a search engine. That is why the keyword resume is placed at the beginning of the search string.

The way it is written, however; de-emphasizes the keyword "resume."

A search string like this would result in a low incidence of resumes.

Initially, by placing the keyword resume at the beginning, you might have perceived it as being the highest weighted word, since it holds the first position. Because of the use of parentheses, however, it is now ranked the lowest.

In this example, the innermost parentheses is **(Oracle OR Sybase)**.

These words will get read first and have a higher ranking. Then they will be matched to Applications or software, which will get the second highest ranking. Then they will be matched to engineer or designer. Finally, the keyword resume will be added, thereby receiving the lowest priority or weight.

Embedded parentheses get read first and then the first word within each parenthesis.

Keyword Positioning and great results

<u>Getting great results from your search string has more to do with keyword order or positioning than selecting and using the right keywords.</u>

This is not to say that electing the keywords is not important. It is! Actually it is very important.

Keyword positioning however, is far more important.

Strategic positioning of your keywords gives you a way to organize keywords into strong search statements. It enables you to make changes within the same query and create keyword groups, and carry out complicated manipulations of the database results. It provides you control to clearly define your search parameters. It provides sharper definition of skills words and carefully selected keywords.

Grouping your keywords and positioning them strategically helps you to structure your query more intelligently. It will help you see which word is causing your results to go astray. It will also help you see how the relevance rankings are been affected by your keywords.

By a simple change in word location you can establish and change meaning and the context of a search string.

Quick ways to Spice up search strings through positioning

To make any kind of serious attempt at effective use of keywords and parentheses through keyword positioning requires creative observation.

Here's a quick tip to guide you.

<u>Monitor your search results as you tweak your search string</u>.

When you run a search string, make it a habit to track the results totals.

Use the data you collect to determine the value of each keyword position.

As you move keywords to different slots in the search string, ask yourself:

Did the number of results increase or decrease?

Did the accuracy of the results improve?

If the accuracy of the results improved you are in the right direction.

Monitoring the results returned as you make changes gives you valuable insights as to what could have gone wrong and how to fix it.

Summing up

Selecting the right keywords is important. More important than the keywords themselves is the positioning within a search string.

You can gain the ability to create new definitions as you see fit. Lastly, you can control relevance scores.

Through well-researched keyword selection and strategic keyword placement, you can boost any search results.

<u>When it comes to crafting search strings efficiently, there can hardly be a more crucial task than positioning keywords appropriately.</u>

The associations that you create through positioning of your keywords are really powerful ways to create vivid word images for the databases. These images allow you to define the framework of any associated concepts the database should use.

Search String Design

The Fourth Pillar of Super Search Strings

Chapter Eight

Getting the most out of your search strings

Step seven – Designing the Right Approach for your Query

So far, we have focused our discussions on keyword related issues. Now we're going to jump into a foundational pillar of search string crafting, which is strategy. More specifically, the approach used to trigger very specific responses from databases.

In a very real way all the previous steps have been leading up to this one.

We have put a lot of effort to create well-crafted queries.

We have...
- Performed thorough keyword research
- Made good decisions about keywords
- Proper keyword selection
- Determining keyword relevance

Let me tell you here, before we go any further, it is not enough.

You can meticulously and strategically select keywords.

You can craft exquisite search strings but when running your search, some of your key assumptions in that wonderfully well written query will go wrong.

The real purpose of your search string

From a recruiting perspective, writing great search strings is a critical skill. In a very real way, your search string is the first, and perhaps the only, chance you will have of finding the right candidate.

The better your search string is, the better your odds of finding the right candidates and getting the hires that you are after.

Without an effective query that turns a database into a Recruiter for you, your database may as well not even exist.

Without solid query writing skills Recruiters will have a hard time sourcing candidates.

When writing queries all Recruiters want the same thing.

The many problems which Recruiters face in search string writing can be reduce to one.

They want lots of candidates, which meet or exceed the qualifications, that are within the targeted location, and that will impress the stakeholders.

These are all great goals, but to get these through your search string you need to engage your database.

Effective vs. Super queries

Writing great search strings doesn't come easily for everyone.

Which is why we need a process to create them.

What is a Super Query?

All the steps that we have discussed so far have turned the search string into an effective one. Effective is good but it isn't enough.

A super search is different than an effective one.

A super query can be long but it doesn't have to be. Super search strings always look simple and obvious. A super search string doesn't just create a great search message to the search engine. A super search string communicates with your database.

Remember: communications is a two way street.

A super search string is base on a dialog between you and your database. I can hear you thinking: "He is really stretching it here."

Effective search string crafting boils down to one thing: defining a clear request in a way that your database has no other option but to deliver it.

Let's just get started....

I always start my searches in Google. I do this even when my query will be designed for my internal database.

My choice to start in Google first is based on a couple of reasons. First, Google provides a preview of all the results that it finds. This helps during my initial scan to review the results before I start clicking on profiles.

The preview also allows me to analyze whether there are any unwanted or irrelevant keywords being pulled in.

The second reason is that Google highlights my keywords to show that it understood. My keywords along with any synonymous concepts that the algorithms might have thrown in for good measure are normally shown in bold.

By having your keywords bolded in the results you are able to form quick judgments.

This can help pinpoint any keyword that may need to be excluded, or any keyword may need to be repositioned.

The process of running your first search on the well-crafted query starts a wave of results from your database or search engine.

When you run a search string on search engine it confronts a slew of elements. These elements create problems that complicate the delivery of results.

You may recognize this search string below:

> resume (Android AND (j2me OR" Java ME" OR JME)) AND (iPhone AND ("Objective C" OR IOS OR OSX OR COCOA OR "COCOA Touch")) AND (OOD OR UML OR "data modeling" OR ERD)

As impressive as looks. It is not a super search string yet. By the way, a super search string doesn't have to be long. It just has to cut thru the clutter of irrelevant results and give you what you need.

Let's try running this search on Google to see how the algorithms respond:

> resume (Android AND (j2me OR" Java ME" OR JME)) AND (iPhone A
>
> Web   News   Images   Shopping   Videos   More ▾   Search tools
>
> About 2,950,000 results (0.81 seconds)
>
> **Texas Senior Iphone Developer Jobs - Find Jobs in the United ...**
> jobs.monster.com › IT › Senior Iphone Developer ▾ Monster ▾
> Jobs 1 - 7 of 7 - Senior **iOS** Developer - **iOS**, **Cocoa**, **Objective-C**, **OOD**/OOP, App D
> ... Email your **resume** to Stanton Apply Job Details Senior **iOS** Developer ... C#) ·
> Strong experience in Java, J2EE, **J2ME**, different **Android** OS versions and.
>
> **Senior iOS Engineer - Work at iHeartRadio**
> jobs.iheart.com/job/senior-mobile-engineering.html ▾ iHeartRadio ▾
> ... code reviews; Designs software using in OOA/D, **UML**, design patterns, **data**

The first thing you'll notice on scanning the results from the above search is the large number of irrelevant results. Due to the billions of pages indexed by search engines like Google, the results usually seem chaotic at times.

This is particularly the case as you write very specific queries that take it away from its comfort zone.

Google is intuitive when it comes to shopping, or checking the weather, or looking for what movie to watch. It stumbles however, when presented with very targeted search strings.

To pull your candidates out of your database, you need to sneak into the mindset of the algorithms. The only way to begin to understand them is to analyze the feedback that they provide.

Pinpointing the candidate is great. Many times that can be good enough.

Until you run your search string in a database or search engine, the strategy needed to achieve the right results won't be revealed.

Once you see what results are returned by your database you will be able to determine what approach will be appropriate one for you search string.

Dealing with Chaotic Results

When Google presents me with bad results I resist the urge to tweak my keywords immediately.

This is where most Recruiters go wrong.

If a Recruiter runs a similar search string they will scroll through see too many irrelevant results and give up on that query. They will just start writing a new search string.

To find the candidates that you need, you must learn to understand when the algorithms are harming your efforts more than helping.

Based on database feedback, your keywords are the means of focusing your database into one single thought:

> "Find my candidate."

The query has some well-chosen keywords; it has strategic keyword positioning, strong use of grouping through parentheses nesting.

In short, it is well structured.

It has to be; we wrote it following our search objective, right?

Even though we specified the need for resumes, among the worse results are included jobs postings, articles, and template resumes.

Before tweaking keyword choices we need to make sure that the search engine algorithms aren't messing with the results.

Irrelevant results don't mean that you used bad keywords. They don't mean that the search string was bad either.

It's useful to look at bad results as a misunderstanding. You thought that you communicated clearly, while you might have inadvertently been unclear about what you needed.

Sometimes we even misuse keywords simply because we didn't realize the impact they would have on our results.

Addressing the issue of irrelevant results is a matter of understanding what the search engine surmised your search intentions to be.

It's amazing how many of the initial assumptions we have about how search strings work is dead wrong. Many times we don't understand what happened so we assumed that the database doesn't have any viable candidates when it was a simple algorithm issue that needed attention.

Identify the right issues

The following are some of the major clues that the results from our search string provide us with:

- Large numbers of results. When the queries return a very large number of results the search engine is telling you that there is something wrong. Either your message is not targeted enough, or the words are weighed by popularity issues.

- Irrelevant or unwanted results – These indicate problems such as bad keyword choice, bad keyword positioning, as well as keyword popularity or prominence.

- Very few resumes scattered and peppered throughout the results. This usually is a sign that the concept of resumes is not emphasized enough.

Anytime you get results that are not exactly what you asked for assumed that there is a misunderstanding. Look for a possible cause for those results and seek to understand what the database's confusion might be.

By understanding the chaos that is the search results, you can pinpoint the underlying causes of search string problems.

Analyzing our results

Upon reviewing our results and comparing it to the three possible scenarios above, we see that resumes are not ranking high enough on our results.

The very first result on the page is a business promoting resumes for contractors, which overshadowed many resumes from individuals below it.

The second is a job posting.

We can deduce that we can address at least two of those possible problems.

The two problems would be:

1. The lack of emphasis on resumes

2. The large number of results

The immediate one would be the need to see resumes.

By confining our search to resumes we can help the keywords make a better impact on our results.

An added bonus from that would be that if we target resumes it would reduce the number of overall results.

Determine an approach

This gives us a purpose to address with our search string. Our search string's purpose now is to cut through the keyword optimized websites and articles and get to the resumes.

Most queries fail because they never really define a correct approach.

Developing your search string purpose will make your keywords act like a magnet to attract the kinds of candidates needed.

With the issues having been identified, now you proceed with the next step.

Let's bring back our initial query:

> resume (Android AND (j2me OR"Java ME" OR JME)) AND (iPhone AND ("Objective C" OR IOS OR OSX OR COCOA OR "COCOA Touch")) AND (OOD OR UML OR "data modeling" OR ERD)

Upon reviewing this query we notice that the keyword resume is deemphasized. This is due to the parentheses nesting. It was given the last scoring and therefore became the least important of the keywords in this search string.

To refocus our search string into resumes we need to emphasize this need.

The Refinement

There is one refinement that we can try here

Refinement: Ask Google to limit the keyword resume to the title or the URL or both. We can do that simply by adding a small search string to our query to look like this:

(intitle:resume OR inurl:resume)

Adding this statement to the beginning of your search string to replace the keyword resume would do two things.

This would create a stronger emphasis two ways.

1. By using parentheses it causes this statement to be read first. This causes the concept of resume to rank higher again.

2. It directs Google to look in those areas that inform it of the keyword prominence. In turn, the results zoom in on the right profiles.

This refinement also indirectly addresses the issues of prominence since it adjusted the relevance scoring.

This may make it unnecessary to tweak for other keyword issues.

Editing and testing your query

This is the point to try our refinements. Here is our new search string:

> (intitle:resume OR inurl:resume)(Android AND (j2me OR "Java ME" OR JME)) AND (iPhone AND ("Objective C" OR IOS OR OSX OR COCOA OR "COCOA Touch")) AND (OOD OR UML OR "data modeling" OR ERD)

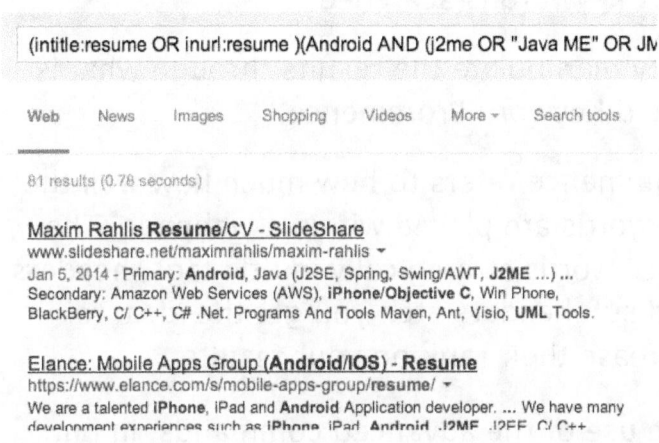

As you can see, adding the refinement brought our results down to a manageable level of eighty-one (81) resumes for us to review.

Refining all search string in this way may not make sense. Sometimes using the keyword "resume" may be enough.

Test each approach until you find the one that works.

Prominence Issues Explained

As it was the case in this query's results, the majority of unwanted results that happen online show up as sites peddling contractors, resume services, or articles that relate to the skill being searched.

Website administrators use prominence techniques to have their site rank first each time your keyword is searched.

They manipulate the results through what is called Keyword Prominence.

Prominence refers to how much how well the keywords are placed within a webpage. They place words strategically in title tags, headers and sub headers etc.; you get the idea, to increase their rank on your results.

The use of the advanced commands, in our search string helped focus the search string by targeting the word resume in those tags.

The commands "intitle" and "inurl" don't always work like they did in our example. When you use them, take a step back and analyze the results.

The results you get will largely depend on how prominently place the other keywords that you search with are.

Another way to get around Prominence

Another approach to our query might be to instead try to reduce the number of results by narrowing using the "filetype:" command.

Document type searches use the three letter file extensions.

Search engines use file extensions to process documents on the web. Without correct file extensions, applications may not be able to properly access or process a file properly.

There are many resumes uploaded on the web with more popping up every day.

Most people save their resumes online in particular formats. The most popularly used ones that come to mind are: doc, pdf, rtf, or even txt.

There may be other but the most popular online resume format, by far, is PDF.

When keywords may be too prominently used in articles narrowing your results thru the use of the "filetype" operator is really effective.

Using the filetype: command asks the search engine to narrow the focus of a query to a particular file extension type.

Let's try an example:

> resume (Android AND (j2me OR"Java ME" OR JME OR "Java Platform, Micro Edition")) AND (UML OR OOA OR OOD) filetype:pdf

```
resume ( Android AND ( j2me OR"Java ME" OR JME OR "Java Platform, I

Web    Videos   Images   News   Shopping   More ▾   Search tools

About 2,950 results (0.53 seconds)

[PDF] Resume Of - Mdc-must.com
www.mdc-must.com/.../173_Hisham%20Mounir%20Ahmed%20Moham... ▾
Database: SQL Server. Mobile Programming: Android. BlackBerry. JAVA-ME.
Windows: ... Documenting and Designing applications with UML. • A good ...

[PDF] Kosta Hristov CV, Short version - Developing the future
www.developingthefuture.net/.../CV/KostaHristov_CV_August_2013_Sh... ▾
by Kosta Hristov - in 24 Google+ circles
ICE Faces, Servlets), Eclipse, SVN, Oracle, JDBC, Hibernate, Ant, , UML, QT,.
```

As complex as this query is it was still able to pull some results all of which were in an Adobe Acrobat PDF format.

There is no guarantee that the resume that you wish to find is in any of these formats but you can narrow the results and cut through prominence issues quickly with this approach.

You can replace the filetype:pdf, command with the following:

> filetype:doc; filetype:txt, filetype:rtf etc...

Why you're going to be better at this than other Recruiters

Quite a few of the keywords and acronyms that we use are heavily affected by prominence issues. These keywords not only form part of job advertisements announcing positions with similar skills, they are also used in articles.

The website administrators work very hard at these types of sites to get their pages and articles to score high on the rankings for your particular keyword.

Every time you search for the same keywords as those highly optimized articles you will experience a problem.

As this pages rise to the top of the rankings, they push the resumes that we are after, way down as well.

The prominence of these keywords in those pages is causing them to overshadow the pages that you really would like to see.

Low prominence scores affect most of the candidates' resumes that we are searching for. This is especially true when considering that the candidates that you are searching for will not be as savvy as those website administrators.

Our prized candidates do not know that the placement of keywords on their online profiles would affect their ranking on results.

They don't have the expertise to get their profile ranking as well as all those articles either.

This makes these resumes with low prominence scores much better targets for us to pursue.

Just think of it!

If we were able to search beyond prominence issues and find these resumes we would have a gigantic advantage over other Recruiters. That is especially so because we won't have many other Recruiters competing with us for these candidates.

You've now got a way to create search strings that define your target skills and that can work their way around the prominence algorithms.

<u>You now have a great competitive advantage!!</u>

It's simple

Assume a low prominence setting for your prospective candidate's resume by default.

Your goal is elevate it to one of great prominence through your search string.

Maximizing your search string

We have tested our search string and it works.

Now what?

Here are some ideas to expand the use of your search strings.

> (Android AND (j2me OR "Java ME" OR JME)) AND (iPhone AND ("Objective C" OR IOS OR OSX OR COCOA OR "COCOA Touch")) AND (OOD OR UML OR "data modeling" OR ERD)

You can already use it as is in your internal database or ATS and should get good results.

If your database asks for a lower number of keywords you may need to tweak it.

The following would be a way to break this string into two:

> (Android AND (j2me OR "Java ME" OR JME))
> AND (OOD OR UML OR "data modeling" OR ERD)

> (IPhone AND ("Objective C" OR IOS OR OSX OR COCOA OR "COCOA Touch"))(OOD OR UML OR "data modeling" OR ERD)

These two queries skill carry the same meaning with fewer keywords.

Yet another way around prominence

Another way to adapt the query is to use it as the base for an x-ray.

Let's add an instruction to focus the search string to LinkedIn:

> site:linkedin.com/in/ (Android AND (j2me OR "Java ME" OR JME OR "Java Platform, Micro Edition")) AND (UML OR OOA OR OOD)

The extra "in" within the search string is not a typo.

This search string is very specific.

This new search string directs Google to look for individual profiles that possess the keywords we targeted.

The 2,180 profiles appear to be the right iPhone developer backgrounds.

Once you understand how prominence works, you're able to recognize the issue, and know how to fix it and make it work for to your benefit.

When you get irrelevant results don't lose sight of your goal. Analyze the database feedback and address the issue.

Addressing Locations

Your search string is a powerful tool. But it's as useless as white crayon if you can narrow results towards a specific location.

While our examples have all focusing skill we have not addressed the issue of narrowing our queries down to geographically. There are several ways to approach it.

The first technique that would accomplish this is to narrow results through zip codes.

As an example let's focus our query to a Dallas, TX:

> resume (Android AND (j2me OR "Java ME" OR JME OR "Java Platform, Micro Edition")) AND (UML OR OOA OR OOD) filetype:pdf (75231 OR 75244 OR 75252 OR Dallas)

Anytime that you introduce number, there is the possibility that the search engine will just pull up that sequence of number in a document, not necessarily interpreted as a zip code.

That is why at the end of the statement I included the word Dallas, as it gives the search engine context to provide better results.

There is no guarantee that it will work but it increases the likelihood that it will.

This next statement focuses on phone area codes in the Dallas area.

> **resume (Android AND (j2me OR "Java ME" OR JME OR "Java Platform, Micro Edition")) AND (UML OR OOA OR OOD) (214 OR 972 OR 682 OR 469 OR Dallas)**

This statement comes with the same warning as the previous one, with one addition. The smaller the number, as in area codes, the higher the possibility that it will pull other number sequences, such as addresses, etc:

This next statement introduces the "numrange" command for Google.

> **resume (Android AND (j2me OR "Java ME" OR JME OR "Java Platform, Micro Edition")) AND (UML OR OOA OR OOD) 75001..75287**

In Google, introducing the two dots between numbers in this manner, you are instructing it to find a number between the two, which you provided.

Narrowing geographically will always cause you problems. Try the different approaches until you find that provides the best results.

As a side note, you can use this same command to do searches that include certification numbers and other numerical based concepts.

Summing up this chapter

This chapter has been all about giving you a real grounding in the way to integrate all the pieces of your queries into a cohesive search string strategy.

We learned that when you first run your search string, some elements that come into play could modify the results. Some can narrow your results too much, others not enough, while another may skew the direction of your keywords.

Here are some of the things we learned.

- Strong choice of words, and clever positioning can't predict whether you will achieve the desired results from your search string.

- Irrelevant results show that there are obstacles to overcome by your queries. The obstacles you face are the things your database does not yet understand. These are the questions that you must answer before you can achieve the results you need. An unanswered question is a barrier to finding.

- The many problems that Recruiters face in search string writing can be reduce to one. Not clearly understanding what they are trying to accomplish with the query.

Don't worry if you are not quick to figure out what is wrong with a search string. You don't need to have everything figured out.

The only way they'll become intuitive in the query writing process is through exposure and practice. Take the time to write queries, add as many keywords as you can.

Avoid using a search string with keywords just thrown together. Be careful, requiring too many keywords or concepts can cause too few results.

It is easy to bring big and meaningful results into your search by incorporating small every day practices. These skills don't come overnight, and they require patience and determination. You have to work smart and hard to acquire them.

As you continue to practice your query writing, you will progress; you will become smarter about your choices with each spin.

Chapter Nine

The Real Purpose of Exclusions

Step 8 – Wiping out irrelevant results

A review of the search string crafting process wouldn't be complete without addressing exclusions in some meaningful way.

Many Recruiters seem to think that searching for resumes is like drinking water with a fire hose.

In other words, run a search string and they drown in unqualified candidates and poor results.

For Recruiters that aren't neck deep in keywords and algorithms, it can be extremely frustrating to see bad results popping up.

For that reason, they rely on exclusions to "clean up" their results.

Adding exclusion statements to your search string has the potential to improve the performance of your queries.

Exclusions offer us some really useful ways to clear out unwanted and irrelevant candidate profiles from our search results. They also can offer us different ways to exercise control over our results.

It's tempting to just start using exclusions. As they can be really helpful but words have many meanings and these can cause you some trouble.

Defining Exclusions

Irrelevant results are one of the greatest concerns for Recruiters searching databases and search engines. This makes exclusions a priority for us to understand.

Let's dig in...

Despite what you may have heard, using exclusion, such as the NOT operator and the minus sign, is not about removing bad keywords.

<u>I know, I can hear you screaming. "What kind of Kool-Aid has he been drinking?"</u>

Exclusions are used for excluding words. I'll give you that. But...

There is no such thing as "bad keywords." Unwanted or irrelevant, absolutely, yes! Bad, not at all.

Exclusions are not a bad way to reduce results but they should be used carefully. Very Carefully.

Exclusions are very powerful tools.

Defining what you expect out of them is especially important to do before you start using them.

Search string surgery

Exclusion can serve you like a scalpel to a surgeon. This is a real appropriate description of exclusions.

A good surgeon would hesitate going straight to a surgery without looking at any other possible alternatives.

This principle holds true of our use of exclusions. The ability to exclude keywords and ideas in strategic ways can make queries very precise.

With exclusions you can help better define your keyword context to your database. The success of your exclusion statement depends on your ability to extract unwanted concepts while refocusing the results from your database.

By using it as a filter to exclude you keywords you can clean up scattered results. Reducing irrelevant results however; should not start with exclusions.

In general, you should shy away from exclusions unless you are absolutely certain there is no context for that term could be relevant for your candidate profile. It should be a last resort method to control irrelevant results from popping up.

Bad results happen because...

Unfortunately yes, sometimes, regardless of how carefully selected, how well placed, and how strategically deployed your search string is, it will still pull bad results.

Bad results can happen for several reasons:

- the elements at play were not understood.
- there was no clear definition of what the search string needed to return
- Sometime they just happen.

Algorithms just get in the way.

The way that algorithms work, every one of your keywords draws in associated keywords. The more associated keywords that they draw in, the less control you have.

To manage the levels of irrelevant results associated with keywords, we use exclusions. They are important because without them we would spend a disproportionate amount of time managing search strings.

Without exclusions, your search results could spiral out of control in several ways.

While using exclusions may seem like it's intuitive. It may not be so much so.

Exclusion Basics

Exclusion is the technique that involves using a word or phrase to filter out irrelevant or unwanted concepts. Negative keywords or exclusions work like a strainer, preventing irrelevant pages from being shown.

After you have decided that a keyword is irrelevant to your search, you can add that term as a negative keyword or exclusion.

The NOT operator is used primarily by databases to perform exclusions. Unlike databases, most search engines accept it but are turning away from it. Now search engines predominantly use the minus sign (–) for that same purpose.

For example:

If you are on a search for resumes online and keep seeing job advertisements. (This happens to be a regular occurrence in the use of search engines.) You could just add the negative keyword job to your search string as follows:

resume Oracle developer –job

This simple search string would to remove those pages in the results that mention the word job.

This would remove some of the unwanted pages.

Words of Caution

A database or search engine will block your keyword from all the results.

In the case of our example, by trying to exclude the job posting, we could well be excluding any possible candidates who used the word job in their profile.

The benefit might overweigh the risk but you have to know that it is a risk just the same.

Exercise caution when using exclusion as you may inadvertently exclude profiles that may still be relevant.

Also, it is important to note that the minus sign in front of words excludes from the results from that particular spelling of your keyword only.

While excluding your word, it allows any variations of your keyword to remain.

In the previous example, the keyword job accompanied by the minus sign excludes any pages that have the word job. Excluding with the keyword "job" doesn't not necessarily clear out all job posting from your results.

That is because not all of the advertisements will use that keyword specifically. When trying to exclude try not to think of just the keyword to exclude but how to affect the results you seek.

A way to get around that is to use other possible variants of your keyword, as shown in the following example:

>resume Oracle developer –job –jobs

The use of the variations here you can cover the exclusion somewhat better. This will normally reduce the amount of job postings in your results dramatically.

While this is a great example of the use of keywords as exclusions, it falls short of the intent. It still doesn't clear out all unwanted job postings.

In the example above, we used the words job and jobs, to emphasize our wish to get resumes.

A better way to accomplish this is to think of words that will isolate the entire concept rather than just a keyword.

Isolating the entire concept of job postings might be easier through the use of the acronym "eoe" as in the example below:

>resume Oracle developer –job – jobs –eoe

This acronym is usually found in job postings to indicate that the company is an equal opportunity employer.

Using the acronym "eoe" as exclusion focuses on the concept of job postings rather than just removing the keyword job.

Adding exclusions in this way may be a better way to tell the database that the job posting results are not what we want.

Together these two acronyms are more effective than each individually.

The process of blocking irrelevant results from your search can be frustrating. Removing them can be slow, and the whole experience exasperating.

While you may not want to use every irrelevant word as exclusion, exclusions can be a useful tool for refocusing your search.

For search efficiency purposes, always spoon-feed your exclusions to your database.

You can't always predict how exclusions will influence your search.

You can't rely on how they will work.

Getting off track

Sometimes as you review search results you will notice some skill words that feel out of topic.

I see it happen

I write what I consider a great search string.

Brilliant, in fact.

A query with all the right components and I feel that it represents my search well. So I run with it.

The results begin well but as I read on something happens.

A lot of the profiles have the right keywords but don't appear to be relevant, not as a whole.

You may not know how but it has gotten off track.

Even the very best queries go off on scattered paths without knowing it sometimes.

I know this from experience.

When I write search strings, I work hard to write a great one so that it will bring the right results the first time.

These scattered results show me that my keywords are associating wrong ideas.

How to tell if you're query is getting off track

At first I had no idea how those off track results were related to the keywords, because I was so fired up about the great search string.

This meant that the results didn't really relate back to my expected results at all. They took off in so many directions that the integrity of the query was completely lost.

It made the results confusing, because I couldn't figure out the main thrust of what I was happening.

To figure out where things are off track, I highly recommend testing your keywords. Rather than giving up on your search string, use those keyword that are off topic as exclusions.

To do so simply attach the minus sign in front of the keyword or keywords and watch for the changes.

If it removes the irrelevant results it means that your keywords are bringing in unrelated concepts.

You may need to research your keywords a little more.

How to test your keywords

Sometimes, when the search string is totally a dud, it is because we gave attributes to a keyword that didn't fit, and therefore, the database didn't connect.

Remember, queries are part of an overall conversation.

Suppose that we were looking for an Oracle developer. Now let us further suppose we were seeing analysts popping up in the results.

For our imaginary role, analyst may be too junior skilled for consideration.

We could exclude by the keyword "analyst". As in the search string below:

    resume Oracle developer –analyst –job –jobs

Analyst as an exclusion may not have been a wise choice as some Oracle developers may have previously held the title of analyst.

Using it as exclusion would remove those profiles as well.

Excluding those off topic words or phrases will give you a way to feel for how keywords are affecting your search and you never know!

They may clean up your results in the process.

Excluding websites

While removing unwanted keywords is by far the most common use to for remove unwanted keywords, it isn't their only use.

Through the use of minus sign as an exclusion device, we can remove websites as well.

When searching the Internet it is not unusual to run across websites that are not pertinent to your search.

An example would be if you kept getting resumes for clients, which you may be restricted from pursuing.

In the example below, we excluded any results that may have ibm.com:

resume Oracle developer -ibm.com

Used this way the minus sign is very useful to quickly solve for results that include my unwanted web site. It's incredibly easy to use exclusions this way, but remember these only remove mentions of these webpages.

This is not the way to remove websites, from your results however; which brings us to a discussion of advanced search commands.

The minus sign and advanced commands

There are two other ways we can use to exclude unwanted web sites.

As you try to block unwanted results, it quickly becomes apparent that you need something more than excluding keywords. Lucky for us that the minus sign can be combined with advanced search commands.

We won't go very deep in our review our review of advanced search commands other than to explain how they can be effectively combined with the minus sign.

The addresses of the Internet today are called url's. The URL is the primary naming scheme used to identify web resources.

Normally websites may include the word job in the url as it indicates where the files and folders are found within a site.

You can use the inurl command to exclude those negative words whenever they may be found in the url as well as in the example below:

   resume programmer JAVA XML VB -tester -inurl:job

This isn't always the case but it works a high percentage of times.

Used this way the inurl command is a great way to increase the relevance of results while helping remove the effects of popular keywords. It also increases the chance of removing job postings. At the same time increasing the likelihood of resumes in the results.

Remove unwanted websites from our results through the use of the inurl command can be easy.

        resume Oracle developer -inurl:ibm.com

This command differs from the previous one in that, -inurl:ibm.com instructs the search engine to just seek out and removes the mention of "IBM.com" in the web address only.

Without the inurl command on the other hand, the search engine would look searches for mentions of the page in the body of the text.

The inurl is tried-and-true technique that can help you write stronger queries. It is effective in removing your unwanted keywords found in the urls.

If you use it wisely, you can use it is a great way to break up irrelevant results from your queries Before you use it in a search string, you need to have a crystal clear idea of what you want it to do.

The Minus Sign and the Site command

The minus sign works well with the site: command for excluding websites as well.

The "site:" command is a bit different from the last two allows commands.

It allows us to find all documents within a website which includes its particular domain. You can also use it to explore all its subdomains, for hidden files not protected behind firewalls.

Let's instruct the search engine to first remove any documents that are hosted on the www.ibm.com servers.

We will type the command like this:

-site:ibm.com

Sometimes you may encounter a web page that ranks high on the results regularly but is irrelevant to you.

By replacing simply the ibm.com with the domain name of the unwanted website you can wipe them it out from the results altogether.

This instruction excludes an entire website from the results. This is a powerful way to remove a website from popping up on your results.

The difference between all three

The difference between using -ibm.com, -inurl:ibm.com, and -site:ibm.com are subtle but important.

   -ibm.com – Using this combination just removes mentions of the word or phrase which may be found anywhere on the pages of your results.

   -inurl:ibm.com – This command target keywords or phrases only when they are found as part of a web address.

   -site:ibm.com – This last command is more powerful as it removes any results that come from the ibm.com website whether they mention IBM or not.

Depending on what you are trying to remove and why each of through these exclusions you can quickly and effectively to adjust the results of your search string.

These three different commands can give you different ways to control the logic of your search string.

As you try them try to understand the type of results each provides and the purpose behind them, and decide at that point what the best one should be.

Excluding Title Tags

There is another well-known command that allows you to search specifically in the title Meta tags and it is rather simply called "intitle."

This command also has specific instructions to the search engines.

It tells the search engine to ignore all other metadata except that found in the title tag.

While it does so, it ignores any instance of the keyword if it is found in the body of the text, or the url or any other location.

The intitle command identifies and returns only documents that contain the word or phrase you specify embedded within the title tags in the web page code.

It is common for web page designers to use the word job in the title tag when uploading an advertisement for jobs.

This makes it a great keyword partnership for Recruiters. Let see how we can use it for exclusions:

-intitle:job

This can excludes job posting that may be inadvertently included along with your keywords.

Word of caution

The format in which you use the minus sign is important to the search engines.

As was mentioned before, spaces are also considered instructions by databases and search engines. This makes spacing between the minus sign very important.

Watch out for your use of spaces when using the minus sign.

In the following query, it is used as a hyphen not an exclusion operator.

HP-UX Oracle

The absence of spaces between the words let's the database or search engine know that this is NOT to be considered a minus sign.

In this instance the change was intentional to signify that the two concepts were united and to be searched together.

Be sure to watch for the proper spacing as you can inadvertently change the Operator to a hyphen.

Unintended spacing between the minus sign and your keyword can trigger irrelevant results to pop up instead.

Chapter Summary

As you create well-refined search strings, exclusions will be a helpful tool to streamline your search strings.

As candidate profiles begin to come back from your search strings, the real query performance trends emerge. You may find specific words within your queries that are generating poor results.

Sometimes, even if you do everything right, search engines can still give irrelevant results. Bad search results is something that happen with any search.

All it takes is one very popular keyword that pulls irrelevant and/or unwanted pages. The point is, bad results can happen even with good keywords.

Keep in mind that you just can't ignore any keyword; if you don't select the exclusion or tell your database or search engine how you will be utilizing them, you might not get the results you are expecting.

Without setting the expectation for the right outcome from your exclusions you will not be able to tell whether it was effective or not.

Knowing how exclusions work and affect your search is key to taking full advantage of them and reducing search time. They can increase your ability to overcome the limitations of your queries.

Be careful to select words that would remove only unwanted results. Otherwise, inadvertently you can exclude some of the skills you wish to find with the wrong use of exclusions. You could lose relevant results.

Having a good set of keywords to exclude with will help you reach and maintain relevant results though your search strings.

To get accurate results you need to do more than exclude keywords. By targeting keywords in titles or in sites or in url's you can have a great tool to counter the effects of keyword popularity, prominence, and keyword density, or frequency which very often derail search results.

As your skill in using exclusions increases, the amount of time it takes of you to achieve the right results will be dramatically reduced.

Remember it is up to you to direct, redirect, and refine the results through the search string. It is up to you to direct the results of your search string into the outcome that you expect to find.

Conclusion

There you have it...

If we had started the book trying to explain a query like the one below, you would have thought it intimidating.

> (intitle:resume OR inurl:resume)(Android AND (j2me OR "Java ME" OR JME)) AND (iPhone AND ("Objective C" OR IOS OR OSX OR COCOA OR "COCOA Touch")) AND (OOD OR UML OR "data modeling" OR ERD) -job -jobs -apply

This is what a super query looks like. Since we built it slowly and methodically, it didn't seem so bad, did it?

The connection between search performance and a strategic keyword driven search has important implications for us as Recruiters.

This is true regardless of whether we are trying to grow professionally, find candidates faster, or trying to be better than our competitors.

The essence of this book has been about giving you the means for translating your keywords into candidates. You have taken in a large amount of information in these chapters.

Throughout it we covered many powerful tools and techniques along with tips to integrate them into search strategies. Incorporating the right techniques into your toolkit is one of the most important, valuable, and high return activities you can undertake.

We learned that searching is not just about getting candidates through your queries, but about getting the right kind of candidates.

You have learned simple steps that can help you get your databases under control and can help you get insight into how it is using your search strings.

We learned that these simple steps could help you build Super Search Strings. These brilliant queries have qualities that no ordinary query has.

A remarkable query can:

- Cut through the chaos of cluttered and unorganized databases and search engines.
- Articulate your search intentions in innovative ways
- Help you leapfrog ahead of the competition.

They all have one thing in common.

They address one or two critical issues in the execution of your keyword statements. They focus and concentrate specific and targeted actions and resources on these pivotal points.

There is a process you can work through to help you write super search strings.

The process follows a series of methodical steps but it involves creativity. That is because you always need to be adapting and redefining the search string you are trying to create.

As a review the eight steps for crafting super search strings are:

1. Creating your search objective
2. Selecting Core Keywords
3. Find the right Supporting Keywords
4. Strengthening queries thru Keyword Stemming
5. Creating word images that target results.
6. Integrating words thru strategic positioning
7. Design the right approach for your query
8. Wipe out Irrelevant Results thru exclusions

Breaking the process into small techniques and building on them helps to create a very specific targeted super search string.

<u>As you can clearly see now, great keywords alone won't do the trick.</u>

Giving your search strings the right focus is a learned skill. It requires a nontrivial grasp of keywords, and a solid idea of what results you're trying to bring about.

The real enemy isn't your query; it's the keyword environment within the search engine.

Crafting strong search strings is subtle. Start with a simple query and then add more complexity. The more that you think through each search string the more you will grasp the nuances that make it work.

The challenge is to ensure that the candidate profiles being returned and keyword targets match best not just a ballpark.

The better that a keyword concepts matches, the more likely it is that you will be getting the right candidate. Remember to keep a balance between keyword accuracy and popularity.

Always keep pressing to embed the insights you've gained into your processes. These insights will help you to better describe to the databases what you need. They will also better equip you to predict how keywords will work. They will also help you to apply them more effectively.

If you endure in this process eventually it will give way to an elegant cycle of feedback and improvements.

Successful search is a product of the number of ideas and the use of appropriate tools to find primary resources of information. It is the practice of looking at how databases, search engines, and words work together to find your candidates that will have a big impact in your search performance.

Make it a habit of building your query and consistently adjusting the approach, ripping it apart and rebuilding, exploring, and taking chances.

Learning to properly unravel such things as keyword specificity, ambiguity etc. will focus your search resources to where the payoff is greater. Only then will your search string amplify the right focus. When it does, your prospective candidate emerges.

Don't let anything deter you from getting the kind of results that you need. Think about it: spending a little bit of time learning and applying these new principles could lead you to large numbers of qualified candidates.

<u>If that is not time well spent. I don't know what is.</u>

Make it your mission to really understand what is happening in your database. Write your own queries. Become familiar with your search objectives.

The methods and techniques to direct your keywords are the same regardless of what different jobs you undertake. You can apply these concepts and enjoy awesome results.

It is possible!

Don't even think that it is beyond your reach.

Many Recruiters are lost and being beaten up by the stress of not being able to find candidates for their roles. The methods that you learned about here are already helping many other Recruiters like yourself, and they can help you too.

I hear from Recruiters all the time and they tell me how much their search has improved. I want to hear from you. I look forward to hearing your success stories.

About the Author

Moises Lopez is the author of "Keyword Search for Recruiters", and now "The Recruiter's Super Query Blueprint."

They are both available at Amazon.com.

Moises is a veteran Recruiter and Sourcing Consultant and renowned trainer in Advanced Sourcing techniques.

He is known for creativity, passion, commitment and results. His passion has driven him to mentoring, training, and helping others share the same success.

He has two decades of experience, both working within corporate and consulting environments building strong relationships as coach and mentor, consistently motivating others toward success. He's trained hundreds of Recruiters to empower their search techniques.

https://twitter.com/Moiseslopez
www.linkedin.com/in/moiseslopez/
http://thesourcingcorner.com
info@thesourcingcorner.com

"Keyword Search for Recruiters"
By Moises Lopez
First Edition: August 2013
ISBN: 149056778X
ISBN-13:978-1490567785

Release date: AUGUST 2013
Media Contact
Moises Lopez
moises@thesourcingcorner.com

Moises does search in ways I have never seen before. He is always on top of the latest and greatest tools for sourcing. Just when you think all avenues have been exhausted, he is notorious for pulling something out of his back pocket to direct your sights on something new.

— Stephanie Hansen-Oldenberg

Accenture

In Keyword Search for Recruiters, Veteran Recruiter and Sourcing Consultant Moises Lopez shares the breakthrough methods for effective searching that he has introduced to hundreds of recruitment professionals across the country.

Moises' premise is simple: Search results are directly proportional to our ability to control the database algorithms. Only when we can control the elements that affect keyword performance can we achieve effective results and unleash the power of search strings.

Keyword Search for Recruiters takes recruitment professionals on a journey of discovery that explains why irrelevant results happen through their search strings and how they can be changed. He breaks down vast amounts of information into interesting narratives that range from keyword performance principles to the applications of Boolean operators and advanced search engine commands.

From core principles to proven tricks, Keyword Search for Recruiters can transform the way you search, showing you how to get results for even the toughest of searches.

Keyword Search for Recruiters:

- Explains the elements that affect keyword performance
- Explores Boolean operators and modifiers
- Covers advanced search engine commands and provides strategies for using them
- Provides the techniques to pinpoint and correct the underlying causes of search string problems in clear, friendly, easy-to-follow language

www.ingramcontent.com/pod-product-compliance
Lightning Source LLC
Chambersburg PA
CBHW051654170526
45167CB00001B/458